Anonymous

The Great Guiteau Trial

With life of the cowardly assassin. A full account! A complete history! The judge's charge to the jury. Speeches of counsel on both sides. Likenesses of all the parties concerned. Guiteau as a theologian, a politician, a tram

Anonymous

The Great Guiteau Trial

With life of the cowardly assassin. A full account! A complete history! The judge's charge to the jury. Speeches of counsel on both sides. Likenesses of all the parties concerned. Guiteau as a theologian, a politician, a tram

ISBN/EAN: 9783337182618

Printed in Europe, USA, Canada, Australia, Japan

Cover: Foto ©ninafisch / pixelio.de

More available books at **www.hansebooks.com**

THE GREAT GUITEAU TRIAL

WITH FULL ACCOUNT
--- AND ---
LIFE OF THE ASSASSIN.

THE GREAT GUITEAU TRIAL:

WITH LIFE OF THE COWARDLY ASSASSIN.

A FULL ACCOUNT! A COMPLETE HISTORY!

THE JUDGE'S CHARGE TO THE JURY.

Speeches of Counsel on Both Sides.

LIKENESSES OF ALL THE PARTIES CONCERNED.

GUITEAU
AS A
"THEOLOGIAN," A POLITICIAN, A "TRAMP LAWYER," "A SOCIETY BEAT," AND AS A MEMBER OF THE ONEIDA COMMUNITY.

PHILADELPHIA:
PUBLISHED BY BARCLAY & CO.,
21 North Seventh Street.

Entered according to Act of Congress, in the year 1882, by
BARCLAY & CO.,
In the Office of the Librarian of Congress, at Washington, D. C.

THE LIFE AND GREAT TRIAL
OF
THE ASSASSIN GUITEAU.

The jury trial is based on the sound principle that the guilt or innocence of a prisoner—his responsibility or irresponsibility—are matters which can be best passed upon by the average common sense of the community. The best argument in its favor comes in great trials like the Guiteau case.

As an humble historian we wish to give our readers one line in preface. Every word herein given is without prejudice. Now let us have one man's opinion on the expert question.

Expert testimony is evidently of but little value in the opinion of Judge Cowling, of the Court of General Sessions, in New York. When a convicted wife murderer was brought up before him for sentence, the prisoner's counsel moved for a suspension of sentence, and the appointment of a commission of medical experts to inquire into his mental condition. The judge denied the motion, remarking that experts could be got to take both sides of any question, and he forthwith proceeded to sentence the murderer to imprisonment for life. This is a good way to prevent the spread of "homicidal mania."

Again we have the other side. You must all remember the great Lefroy case —the murder of Mr. Gould in an English railway carriage. A jury having convicted him, and it being clear that he was of sound mind, or responsible for his actions at the time he committed the crime, no attention was paid to the plea that insanity was hereditary in his family. When he had confessed not only this, but another cold-blooded murder, the very enormity of his offences gave rise to the theory that he was possessed with a homicidal mania, but this did not save him. If such a doctrine should ever prevail, the more diabolical a man's crimes might be the better would be his chances of escape from punishment in this world. The English authorities did not adopt that doctrine, however. They hanged Lefroy.

Garfield's Thoughts on the Insanity Plea.

In 1871, a murder trial took place in Cleveland, the defence being insanity. Judge R. F. Payne was on the bench, and his charge was a complete annihilation of the shallow pretence upon which the plea of insanity is often sustained. A few days afterward Judge Payne received the following letter from Garfield

"Dear Judge:—Allow me to congratulate you on your splendid charge to the jury at the close of the Gelentine case. The whole country owes you a debt of gratitude for brushing away the wicked absurdity which has lately been palmed off on the country as law on the subject of insanity. If this thing had gone on much further all that a man would need to secure himself from the charge of murder would be to rave a little and tear his hair a little, and then kill his man. I hope you will print your excellent charge in pamphlet form and send it to all the judges in the land.

"Very truly yours,
JAMES A. GARFIELD."

Worthy of attention also is a letter dated at Washington, D. C., and written by the well-known journalist, editor and publisher, Watterson, written to his own paper, the Louisville (Ky.) *Courier-Journal*, in which he says:

"Accident rather than curiosity drew me towards Judge Cox's court rooms, where I spent this forenoon. The effect upon my mind amounted to a complete reversion of opinion and feeling. I had imagined the trial a farce; it is a tragedy. I had dismissed Guiteau from consideration as a muddy-mettled 'knave and fool.' He impressed me to-day as a man of acute understanding, and, though a blundering, a truculent wit. I sat close to him; could see every glance of his eye, every phase of his expression, the slightest detail of poise and gesture. The man is an excellent actor. He has a capital stage grimace and laughter. I declare there were times when he actually captivated me by his well-timed interpositions and effective by-play. I came away precisely as one who had witnessed a stirring act in an eccentric drama, wherein all the parts were well played.

"Guiteau, to begin with, could not have played his part better. Of course he overdid it, because the mimic world and the real world cannot be made to harmonize; but, as a mimic actor on a real stage, he certainly cuts no mean figure, and will go down to history as absolutely *sui generis*—a sort of weird and wizened apotheosis of dead-beatism. All descriptions of his personal appearance are at fault. He is simply brazenly and shabbily and scantily genteel. His voice, instead of being harsh and unnatural, is both trained and taking; not resonant like the voice of Voorhees; not cultivated to the pitch of Wendell Phillips, but a homely, a vulgar cross between the two, with a touch of *Mulberry Sellers* and a reminiscence of *Rip Van Winkle*. He is no more crazy than I am. He shot Garfield as the last desperate venture in a life of moral obliquity and personal discomfiture.

"All the other parts in this startling extravaganza are well impersonated. Judge Cox certainly presides with dignity, and, considering *pros* and *cons*, I cannot see how he could have avoided this droll pageant. On the whole, I think Corkhill leads the prosecution exceedingly well, and has the case thoroughly in hand. He thinks he is sure of a verdict and I agree with him. It is impossible for anybody to see this exhibition and come away without being satisfied that, morally, legally, intellectually and sentimentally Guiteau deserves to be hanged, and will meet no other fate."

And now as to the trial. Our experience of over forty years in the getting up books of this character proves that the readers prefer, first a concise and direct account of the trials, and are particularly out of patience with reiterations and of a report in detail of witness after witness who but repeats the testimony of the preceding one. Therefore, we give you first a complete and connected account, and *follow* it with the "side issues" of this great case.

The Trial.

The trial of Charles J. Guiteau for the murder of James A. Garfield, President of the United States commenced in the District Supreme Court, Washington, D. C., before Judge Cox, on Monday, November 14th, 1881. District Attorney Corkhill, and Messrs. Porter and Davidge, for the prosecution; Scoville (Guiteau's brother-in-law) and Robinson for the defence (who afterwards withdrew). After Guiteau was brought in, the district attorney announced that the Government was ready to proceed. Mr Robinson asked for more time—a request opposed by the other counsel for the prisoner, (Mr. Scoville,) and by Guiteau himself, who insisted on being heard. Judge Cox directed that the case should proceed. The selection of jurors was commenced, and five were obtained.

The Second Day

was taken up entirely with the selection of jurors. There was so much challenging by the Government and the defence, that only four more jurors were secured.

On the Third Day,

The three jurors needed were obtained. The completed jury is as follows:
1. John P. Hamlin, restaurant keeper.
2. Fred. W. Brandenburg, cigar dealer.
3. Henry J. Bright, retired merchant.
4. Charles J. Stewart, merchant.
5. Thomas H. Langley, grocer.
6. Michael Sheehan, grocer.
7. Samuel F. Hobbs, plasterer.
8. George W. Gates, machinist.
9. Ralph Wormley, colored laborer.
10. W. H. Brauner, commission merchant.
11. Thomas Heinlein, ironworker.
12. Joseph Prather, commission merchant.

On this day Guiteau issued an appeal "to the legal profession of America" asking legal aid in his case from "any well-known lawyer of criminal capacity."

The Fourth Day.

The court room was thronged with a distinguished audience drawn thither to listen to the evidence of Secretary Blaine. Guiteau's inordinate vanity ascribed the brilliant gathering to his own importance, and looked highly pleased and gratified. The Secretary of State gave his testimony at length, and was subjected to a rigid cross-examination in reference to the political situation at and just preceding the time that President Garfield was assassinated. After Secretary Blaine's examination, Guiteau broke out in a diatribe against his counsel. After the Judge had silenced him, Mr. Simon Camacho, the Venezuelan minister, who had waived his diplomatic privilege and appeared as a witness, gave a description of the scene at the depot on the morning of the shooting. In his cross-examination the witness explained how the prisoner wore his hat, and Mr. Scoville placed Guiteau's hat upon his (Guiteau's) head, partly on the side. Witness stopped the counsel, saying, "That is the way he wore his hat." Guiteau said, "That is false; I wear my hat this way," placing it on his head perfectly straight. He added: "I wear my hat this way, and do not go sneaking around." The minister was interrogated further, but nothing further elicited.

Mrs. Sarah B. White, matron of the Baltimore and Potomac depot ladies' waiting-room, was next called. She explained the circumstances of the shooting in detail, substantially as published in her statement obtained soon after the shooting. She recognized Guiteau as the person who fired the shot. She had seen the prisoner walking up and down the gentlemen's rooms previous to the arrival of the Presidential party on the morning of July 2d. She did not observe the pistol in the assassin's hand when she went to the President's assistance. "Guiteau," she said, "was only about three feet back of the President when he fired at him."

Cross-examined—Witness saw nothing remarkable in the prisoner's appearance, excepting that he walked to and fro in the gentlemen's room, keeping his eyes constantly on the ladies' room, as if waiting the arrival of some one.

Robert A. Parke, ticket agent of the Baltimore and Potomac Railroad Company at Washington, testified that he saw Guiteau on the morning of the 2d of July; witnessed the firing of the second shot by the prisoner; rushed from his office out into the corridor, and, as Guiteau was fleeing, seized him and kept hold of him until relieved by the police officers. In his cross-examination Mr. Parke recited in detail his statement of the circumstances of the shooting, and said that the prisoner was moving very rapidly when he seized him. He explained that the prisoner mentioned several times that the letter to General —— would explain everything.

Judson W. Wheeler, of Virginia, described the details of the shooting. The firing occurred but a short distance from him. So close was it that he inhaled the smoke from the revolver, which caused him to cough.

George W. Adams, publisher of the Washington *Evening Star*, was the next witness called. He testified that after the first shot was fired the President raised his arms. At the second shot the President sank gradually to the floor. He saw the man who fired the shot run. Cross-examined—Mr. Adams said that the prisoner did not appear to be hurrying to get away. He understood Guiteau to say several times that it was all right. He observed the prisoner's countenance, but was not impressed with it as indicating excitement. The whole matter, he thought, occurred in about ten seconds. He mistook the prisoner for a countryman trying to pacify the passengers.

The last witness of the day was Jacob P. Smith, the janitor of the railroad depot. He detailed the circumstances of the shooting, but insisted that it was the second shot that took effect.

On the Fifth Day,

Guiteau, directly after the opening of court, made another violent verbal attack on his lawyer, Mr. Scoville. He was silenced by the Judge threatening to have him removed and the trial continued.

Miss Ella M. Ridgely, a young lady, testified that she was at the depot on the morning of the 2d of July. She gave a more circumstantial account of the shooting than any witness yet. She saw the prisoner making the contract with the hackman to drive him to the cemetery, and then in the ladies' waiting-room with his hand in his pocket. He drew out a weapon, and the witness noticed the sunlight shining on the barrel, although she did not realize, at that moment, that it was a pistol. A first shot was fired, and then the prisoner took two or three steps nearer to the President, and fired a second shot when about four feet from him. On the first shot the President threw up his hands and half fell back. He kept sinking all the time as the second shot was fired. She was not sure whether the second shot touched him at all.

William S. Crawford, a wagon-driver, saw the firing; could not see the President, but distinctly saw Guiteau aim and fire, and saw his arrest.

John R. Scott, special officer on duty at the depot, was at the south gate when the first shot was fired. At the second shot he ran in the gate and across the hall, and saw Mr. Parke holding Guiteau. He (Guiteau) said: "I will go to jail, but I want General Sherman to have this letter." On the way Guiteau said: "I'm a Stalwart, and Arthur is now President."

District Attorney Corkhill then handed the pistol to the witness, who identified it as the one taken from the prisoner. There was a noticeable stir in the court room and a craning of necks in every part of the room, with the whispered exclamation: "There's the weapon that killed poor Garfield!" The pistol was handed around and examined by the jury—their attention being called to the fact that two barrels were empty and four were still loaded.

Policeman Kearney testified at great length, and described the arrival of the President at the depot and of his movements. He heard the shot fired, and rushed to the door of the station, but before he could mount the steps he heard another shot and a scream. Just afterward Guiteau rushed out and right into his arms. The prisoner said he wanted to send a letter to General Sherman; but Kearney held on to him, when he struggled to break away, and the officer drew his club to strike him, but soon subdued him without violence. As he was proceeding with the prisoner Kearney says Parke came up and said: "I arrest you for shooting the President;" but, as Guiteau was already in custody, his observation was superfluous, and Kearney contradicted Parke's statement that he first arrested Guiteau. Kearney was then assisted by officer Scott, and they took the prisoner out of the depot, when Guiteau said: "I did it; I will go to jail for it; Arthur is President, and I am a Stalwart!"

John Taylor (colored), a hack driver, testified to a conversation with Guiteau relative to taking him to the cemetery from the depot. It was about a week previous to the shooting.

While waiting for a witness Mr. Scoville arose and said: "I give notice now that the defence in this case is insanity, and we will claim that the burden of proof is on the prosecution. If they intend to introduce evidence on that point they must introduce it before they close."

Mr. Davidge. We think otherwise, and we will act according to our own convictions of what is proper. The defence has made no opening.

Mr. Scoville. I give you notice now

The entire police force of Washington and U. S. troops in readiness to protect Guiteau on his way to and from the court.

Die ganze Polizei-Force von Washington nebst dem Militair wird aufgeboten, um Guiteau auf seinem Wege nach und vom Gerichtssaale zu schützen.

before you close your proofs; I simply want to make it a matter of record.

Judge Cox. I understand.

Sevillon A. Brown, chief clerk of the State Department, was next sworn, and testified to Guiteau's visits to the department and his application for the Paris consulship.

J. Stanley Brown, private secretary to the late President Garfield, testified relative to Guiteau's visits to the White House. His first visit was early in March, and his visits were repeated at intervals of two or three days until the first of June. Witness identified several letters and notes handed to him by the District Attorney as those which had been left at the White House by Guiteau. The question of identifying the letters being discussed, Guiteau broke in again with: "They are all right; I wrote them all."

When Mr. Brown was asked if Guiteau was always treated with courtesy at the White House, and replied in the affirmative, Guiteau added: "You should rather say cordially."

The letters referred to by Mr. Brown were read.

The last witness of the day was James L. Denny, who had charge of the news-stand at the depot, and received some papers from Guiteau on the morning of the shooting.

On the Sixth Day

The crowd about the court house was far greater than upon any former day. At half-past nine o'clock all the corridors leading to the court room were densely packed, and it was with the greatest difficulty that those whose presence was needed in the court room could gain admission. To avoid an inevitable scramble it was found necessary to issue tickets of admission. These were given out from the marshal's office, and only ticket-holders were permitted to enter. At twenty minutes before ten the doors were opened, and in a few minutes every seat was occupied.

The larger portion of the spectators were ladies. Guiteau arrived at the court house at nine o'clock, and, without any particular demonstration on the part of the crowd, was taken at once to the prisoner's room, where he ate a hearty breakfast and expressed himself well satisfied with the progress of his case.

Mr. Scoville was questioned in relation to Guiteau's alleged new counsel—Judge Magruder, of Maryland—and stated that he was not aware of any tender of services from Judge Magruder; that he had received several offers from lawyers who were strangers to him, but feared he might make a great mistake by taking on strangers at that stage of the case. He did not expect to have any other assistance than that of Mr. Robinson, the counsel assigned by the Court.

The court was opened without incident, and George C. Maynard, electrician, was put on the stand and testified to loaning Guiteau ten dollars at one time and fifteen dollars at another.

Guiteau protested against the line of evidence; did not think it anybody's business whether he owed twenty-five dollars or some one owed him. "Maynard is a good fellow, and I owe him twenty-five dollars; that's all there is in it."

District Attorney Corkhill desired to prove by the witness that Guiteau borrowed the fifteen dollars with which he bought his revolver.

On cross-examination witness thought Guiteau looked seedy and hungry. The prisoner showed much feeling, and frequently interrupted the witness, asserting that he lived in first-class style and wore a mild suit of clothes. He knew plenty of public men, and had all the money he wanted. His mental condition, and not physical, was at fault. He had a big load on his mind about that time. Witness did not notice anything particular about his manner except

A Sort of Skulking Gait.

James N. Burkart, clerk to Mr. Maynard, also testified to the loan of the fifteen dollars, and thought Guiteau's walk and the way he held his head a little peculiar.

John O'Meara testified to selling the pistol to Guiteau. He could not identify it, as there were thousands just like it. The charges were then drawn from the revolver at the suggestion of counsel, much to the relief of the audience.

Pending the examination of the pistol

THE GREAT GUITEAU TRIAL.

Guiteau desired to announce to the Court that he invited John B. Townsend, of New York, and Leonard Swett and U. S. Trude, of Chicago, to assist him. There was plenty of brains on the other side and he desired as much on his, in the interest of justice. Another matter, he continued, "I desire to call to the attention of the Court. There are a number of disreputable characters about the court and some threats of violence have been made during the week past. I have no fears for my personal safety. The chief of police has kindly furnished me a body-guard, and I wish to notify all evil-disposed persons that if they attempt to harm me my body-guard will shoot them down. That's all there is about it." Then nodding to the reporters' table, he added, "Reporters, put that down."

Colonel A. S. Rockwell, the next witness, began to detail the occurrences at the depot when Mr. Scoville interposed, acknowledging the killing. Guiteau quickly shouted: "No, your Honor, we acknowledge the shooting, but not the killing." Colonel Rockwell briefly stated the facts within his knowledge, and without cross-examination was followed by General D. J. Swaim. Witness was at Elberon when the shooting occurred.

Dr. D. W. Bliss was then called. He gave a narrative covering from the time he was called to the President's side, (fifteen or twenty minutes after he was shot,) until his death. The immediate cause of his death was hemorrhage. Witness then explained minutely the character of the wound, using the upper portion of a wired skeleton for the purposes of illustration, and detailed at great length the progress and symptoms of the case. Pending the arrival of the fractured vertebræ—which the district attorney announced had been sent for—witness was subjected to a lengthy cross-examination, the supposed object being to lay a foundation for the theory of malpractice, which Guiteau insisted must be made the foundation-stone of his defence. Quite the sensation of the trial was produced when the district attorney suddenly drew from a pasteboard box upon his table a section of a human backbone, and, holding it up, inquired: "Do you recognize this, Doctor?" The audience hung breathless upon the answer, as the witness, in measured tones, replied: "I do. It is a portion of the vertebræ of the late President, James A. Garfield." The vertebræ were then handed to the jury, and the character and extent of the injury to them was explained by the witness.

The witness was followed with the closest attention on the part of the entire audience with the sole exception of Guiteau, who devoted himself to his papers, only occasionally glancing up with the air of a man being bored with a recital in which he could have no possible interest.

After the vertebræ had been returned to the district attorney's table, Mr. Scoville reached over and requested an opportunity of examining it. It was handed to him, and Guiteau who sat immediately on his right examined it closely as Mr. Scoville turned it over and from side to side. He made no move to touch it, however, and gave not the slightest indication of any feeling other than a casual curiosity.

The examination of the witness was continued until the hour of recess arrived.

Upon the reassembling of the court Dr. Bliss again took the stand, and the cross-examination of the witness was conducted by Mr. Scoville. Before the recess the examination was managed by Mr. Robinson, who read his questions from manuscript. The ingenious and comprehensive scope of his examination plainly suggested the handiwork of some medical expert. At one point the witness used the term "aneurism." "Please explain to the jury what that is," said the district attorney; "I don't know what it is." Counsel for the defence smiled sympathizingly, when the district attorney retorted: Oh! we see very clearly that you understand all about it."

Witness was requested by Mr. Robinson to detail the symptoms and treatment day by day during the course of the President's illness, and read from the records of the case as prepared by the surgeons in charge. The notes being in the handwriting of Dr. Reyburn, the latter was sworn, and took his place by the side of Dr. Bliss to assist as interpreter.

After the witness had consumed twenty

minutes in reaching the records of three days, counsel for the prosecution interposed an objection to the course of the examination.

Mr. Davidge, for the prosecution, judged from the questions asked that the defence proposed to set up the theory of malpractice. He denied their right at this point and upon the cross-examination of the witness—who had upon his examination in chief simply testified to the character of the wound—to lay the foundation of the theory. He proposed to place in the hands of the defence the full records from which the witness had been reading, and thus save the time of the Court.

The defence yielded to the suggestion, and Mr. Robinson continued the examination of the witness, closely questioning him as to the autopsy.

Questioned by Mr. Davidge, Dr. Bliss stated that the main element of danger from a wound of the character described was from the injury to the backbone and from the lacerating of the splenic artery, which latter of itself must eventually necessitate death. The wound was a mortal wound.

At this point in the evidence Guiteau, who, since the recess, had been quietly reading a paper, leaned forward with a nervous movement and wrote rapidly for a few moments.

The examination of Dr. Bliss having been concluded, the district attorney inquired of the defence if they proposed to pursue the same course of examination with the rest of the medical witnesses, and Mr. Robinson replied, "About the same." Guiteau here attempted to say something, when the district attorney, bowing with mock gravity, continued: "If Mr. Guiteau will permit me, your Honor, I will move an adjournment." Guiteau appeared to relish the pleasantry, and, nodding, replied: "Oh, certainly; you shall have full chance."

The Court then adjourned.

Guiteau Shot at.

Three attempts were made about this time to kill Guiteau. One attempt by a soldier named Mason, who was said to have been under the influence of liquor at the time. The most sensational attempt of three we give a spirited illustration of, and below a faithful account of it. The party was a young farmer living not far from Washington, one Jones by name.

Upon the adjournment of the Court on Saturday, November 19th, the van started as usual for the jail, having one policeman as a guard, who sat on the seat with the driver. Before reaching the Capitol, the guard noticed a young man on horseback riding leisurely behind the van. Near the corner of East Capitol and First street, the horseman rode directly up to the rear of the van, and hastily peered through the small grating. Guiteau was alone in the van, and seated on the right-hand side, the seats running lengthwise of the van. After evidently satisfying himself of the location of the prisoner, the horseman wheeled suddenly to the right of the van, and fired directly through it. He then dashed to the front of the van, and pointed his pistol at the driver, with the evident intention of intimidating him, or stopping the van. The driver was somewhat excited, and, in response to an inquiry of the reporter, said perhaps he intended to stop the van by shooting one of the horses. Seeing an armed policeman by the side of the driver, he exclaimed: "I've shot the — of a —!" and putting spurs to his horse, dashed down East Capitol street in the direction of the Congressional Cemetery. The policeman fired one shot at the fast-disappearing horseman and the driver of the van whipped his horses into a gallop, and kept in sight of him for several blocks. The would-be avenger was, however, mounted upon a blooded horse, and readily escaped out into the country. He was described as a smooth-faced man, about twenty-five years of age, and a dashing horseman. He had on a dark-brown suit of clothes. The van then proceeded to the jail, and Guiteau was taken out in a state of great excitement. He exclaimed: "I have been shot! Notify Major Brook at once. Tell him to arrest the scoundrel, and have him dealt with as he deserves!"

On examination it was found that the ball had just grazed Guiteau's left wrist, inflicting a mere scratch. The ball struck the opposite side of the van and fell on the floor, where it was found on reaching the jail.

THE GREAT GUITEAU TRIAL.

The announcement of the attempt on Guiteau's life created intense excitement upon the streets, and all sorts of rumors were at once in circulation. Jones was seen about the court house and attempted to gain admission during the day, but failed. He was also seen to mount his horse near the court house soon after the van left and ride leisurely after it.

Both Mason and Jones were arrested and held to answer. The first attempt was by a guard in the jail who tried to get at him with a knife but was secured in time to save the "theologian."

The seventh day of the trial Judge Cox became weary of the prisoner's impertinent interruptions, but gave him, none the less, full sway.

Dr. Henry P. Stearns again took the stand, and Mr. Scoville resumed cross-examination. He stated, in reply to Mr. Scoville, that the faculty of memory was generally the first to show impairment in most all forms of insanity. Sometimes, however, and in some cases, the memory might be unusually active and retentive.

Mr. Scoville asked: "Do you agree with the last witness that insanity is always the outward manifestation of a diseased brain?"

Judge Porter objected to the form of question, and insisted that the defence should observe the same rule that the prosecution had adhered to, of letting each witness tell what he knew.

Guiteau—You are getting excited.

Mr. Scoville—I must say Judge Porter can make the most out of nothing of any man I know.

After further questions relative to brain disease, Mr. Scoville asked: "Is it true that such disease of the brain can always be detected by an examination of that organ?"

Answer—I can only answer you that there have been cases of disease of the brain where upon examination after death no lesion of the brain has been detected.

The witness was about to make some observations just as Mr. Scoville proposed another question, when Judge Porter said (to the witness): "Go on, Doctor, and finish your answer."

Mr. Scoville—Well, hold on a minute! We would like to know who is conducting this examination—you, or I?

Judge Porter—I assume that the Court is conducting it, and to the Court I shall always appeal for an enforcement of the practice. The witness is one of the most noted scientists of this country, and you must not attempt to treat him as though he was your schoolboy. I will not permit it.

Mr. Scoville (with some warmth)—Well, let us see about it, Mr. Judge Porter!

Guiteau chimed in with a hit at Judge Porter, but without raising his eyes from a pamphlet which he was pretending to read. A broad grin overspread his features, and he seemed to enjoy greatly the storm of angry words.

Judge Cox, however, interposed with a few smooth words, which turned away the wrath of counsel, and the examination proceeded without incident.

When Judge Porter again protested that Mr. Scoville should not be permitted to rebuke the witness, Mr. Scoville said: "I can see no occasion for your speech. I have neither rebuked the witness, nor had occasion to do so."

Guiteau—What's the matter with you, Porter, any way? You must have contracted Davidge's disease during the night.

Mr. Scoville began to read from manuscript what appeared to be a hypothetical proposition.

Mr. Davidge (with mock bewilderment) interrupted: "Oh! come! come! Mr Scoville, I can't understand that!"

Mr. Scoville (laughing)—Well, I don't understand it myself. Mr. Reporter, please erase that, and I will put another question.

Colonel Reed then put a few questions to the witness in rapid order.

Judge Porter again interposed an objection, and, in a highly dramatic manner, demanded that the witness should be allowed to finish his answer, and not be cut short by the counsel.

Colonel Reed—The witness has not intimated any desire to say anything further in reply to that question. You are the one who appears to be anxious for more. (To the witness)—Doctor, do you desire to add anything to your reply?

Witness—No, sir. I thought I answered the question directly and sufficiently.

Colonel Reed—As I supposed. Judge Porter, you disagree with your own witness, as usual. (General laughter at the expense of Judge Porter.) (Aside to Mr. Scoville)—He will get over it after a while. The examination progressed with frequent objections on the part of the prosecution, and requiring the ruling of the Court.

As the witness was about to retire Guiteau said: "Allow me to ask if you hold the opinion that a man cannot be insane in a specific act without having a disease of the brain?"

Mr. Scoville assented to the question, and witness replied that insanity meant disease of the brain.

Guiteau asked another question, but Judge Porter suggested to the witness that he hold no conversation with the criminal.

Guiteau (angrily)—I'm no criminal any more than you are. I'm here as my own counsel, and I have as much right to speak as you have. Wait till I am convicted before you call me a criminal. I stand a great deal better than you do. Plenty of men will say I'm a bigger man than old Porter.

Colonel Corkhill suggested that if this abuse was permitted the prosecution would insist that the prisoner be removed to the dock.

Judge Cox—The Court has already considered the advisability of such a course.

Guiteau—The Court has no discretion in the matter. I appear here as my own counsel in accordance with the law and usage in every State in the country.

The incident was evidently without any effect upon the prisoner, who seemed to realize—now that he has boldly asserted that he is perfectly sane—that he will be held amenable to the same rules of behaviour as other sane people.

Dr. Jamin Stron, of Cleveland, O., visited the jail, and investigated the mental and bodily condition of the prisoner. As he was about to state the results of his examination Guiteau looked up and said: "Doctor, let me cut this short by saying, I'm in good physical condition, and as sane as you are. There's a great deal of useless rubbish being dragged into this case. Let's cut it short."

Judge Porter arose, and again demanded the interference of the Court to put a stop to the interruptions on the part of the prisoner.

Mr. Scoville replied: "The counsel on this side will assent cheerfully and readily to any proposition you may make. Only make your proposition. Don't make your little speeches to the jury now."

Judge Porter (with much excitement)—You have insulted a distinguished gentleman upon the witness-stand, and now you assume to dictate the management of our case.

At this point Guiteau again lost his temper and discretion, and shouted back at Judge Porter, while the latter addressed the Court in his most impressive manner. For a few minutes neither could be distinctly understood.

Judge Cox finally secured silence, and stated that, while he did not desire to act hastily, he should punish for contempt if the prisoner again transgressed the bounds of propriety.

Guiteau—Very well, Your Honor. I am within the discretion of the court, but I do not appear here as an ordinary criminal, and Your Honor recognizes it. I appear as my own counsel, and have so acted for the past six weeks.

Colonel Reed then proposed the hypothetical case of the defence, and asked if witness could give an opinion.

Witness evaded a direct answer, and counsel insisted upon a categorical reply. A sharp colloquy ensued between Judge Porter and Colonel Reed, with side remarks by Guiteau, such as: "Porter, you got a mouth like a catfish!" and shortly afterward: "Porter, you'll bring up in a lunatic asylum yet!"

Judge Cox ruled that the counsel for the defence could require a categorical answer, and the question was again and again put, but each time witness insisted upon qualifications which evaded a direct answer.

Guiteau sneeringly remarked· "You are the stupidest fellow we've had yet!"

Colonel Reed finally said: "Well, if you cannot answer the question, you may step aside."

Guiteau shouted after the witness: "Now go and get your five hundred dollars and go home!"

Dr. Abram M. Shew, superintendent of the Connecticut Hospital for the Insane, at Middletown, Conn., was the next witness. He had held the position for fifteen years, and had previously for fifteen months, acted as assistant physician at the asylum at Auburn. In the course of the examination the witness stated that among insane criminals egotism, great vanity and ignorance were marked characteristics. The witness stated that he had made two examinations of the prisoner at the jail, for the purpose of discovering his mental and physical condition, and had noticed the conduct of the prisoner in court since November 28th; and he had formed the opinion that the prisoner is sane.

Guiteau—Sane now; but insane on the 2d of July.

Colonel Corkhill then asked: "Assuming the facts set forth in the hypothetical question which you have heard read to be true, do you think that he was sane or insane on the 2d of July?"

Guiteau—"He don't know anything about it."

Witness—"I think he was sane."

After recess Colonel Reed conducted the cross-examination of the witness.

Guiteau interrupted once, and, with some excitement, said: "These experts may all be very honorable men, but I don't care a snap for their testimony. I wouldn't give a cent a bushel for it, whether for me or against me."

Judge Cox—"Be quiet, prisoner; you have promised to keep still."

Guiteau—"All right, Judge, but I wanted to get that idea before the jury."

Witness stated that he did not think the prisoner had been acting a part or feigning in court. He thought he had been acting purely according to his natural characteristics.

Dr. Orpheus Evarts, superintendent of the private insane asylum at College Hill, Ohio, was then called. He said: "There is no uniformity of head, either as regards size or form, either in sane or insane people. The expression of the face, while some indication, is in no case a sure indication in determining the sanity or insanity of a person." Witness had examined the prisoner in the jail, had conversed with him, had closely watched his conduct during the trial, and had formed the opinion that the prisoner on the 2d of July was sane.

Objection was made by Mr. Scoville and overruled, and exceptions noted.

Guiteau—This is all rubbish—all this nonsense to prove that I am sane now—and it has nothing to do with the 2d of July. These experts have seen me since the trial began. I don't claim now, and didn't claim when they saw me, to be insane: consequently they assume that I was sane on the 2d of July. It's all nonsense!

Upon cross-examination, witness stated —I did not believe the prisoner was shamming, in the sense of feigning insanity. I do not believe him to be sincere, but I do not think he has been feigning insanity in court.

Mrs. Scoville next took the stand. Mr. Scoville stated that he desired to ask her a few questions now, as owing to sickness in their family, it was necessary for her to return home at once. She identified a letter written by her father in 1875, in which he said: "Charles is crazy, and should be in an asylum."

Colonel Corkhill desired, as Monday (the day following Christmas) would be a legal holiday, to have an adjournment till Tuesday, which was so ordered, and the Court then adjourned to that time.

As the audience arose to leave, Guiteau shouted: "To-morrow being Christmas, I wish the Court and the jury, and the American people, a happy Christmas. I'm happy, and I hope every one else will be."

During that week the Guiteau "circus" was continued, with much amusement and "roars of laughter" among the audience. The demand for places at the trial was so overwhelming that it required a platoon of police to repress the eager public. The business of the week was the determination of Colonel Corkhill, the prosecutor, to prove that insanity was not a peculiarity of the Guiteau family.

Poor Mr. Scoville, the assassin's counsel, had a very sad time and deserved the sympathy of all good citizens. Doing what he considered (right or wrong) his duty, he was kept in a constant broil with his wretched brother-in-law, opposed by the best legal talent of the country, without a chance to make either reputation or money by the process. Yet he stuck to his task heroically.

The business of the court repeated

Guiteau "rises to object," gets off his "funny remarks," and is requested to "sit right down again." Showing the great patience of Judge Cox.

Guiteau „erhebt Einwand," macht einige „seiner scherzhaften Bemerkungen" und setzt sich auf Geheiß sofort wieder auf seinen Platz. Ein Beweis für die Lammesgeduld des Richters Cox.

itself during the week, and may be summarized briefly in some of Guiteau's "cranky" outbursts.

Guiteau objected to witnesses giving his history and the story of his peculiarities in business. He burst out, in spite of his counsel, and precipitated a "scene." The Court, however, ruled that all such evidence was admissible.

The witness, Rev. R. S. McArthur, pastor of Calvary Baptist Church, New York, who was called to give some idea of the business methods, crazy or otherwise, of the prisoner, was frequently interrupted by Guiteau. The witness said he never saw any indications of insanity in any member of the Guiteau family.

On this the assassin sprang to his feet, and shaking his fist at the reporters' table, said, after a long and crazy declamation: "You fellows have been making out this case to suit yourselves. You have been sending on scandalous reports to your papers; but I'll have you all hauled over for it." As for Dr. McArthur, the witness, Guiteau expressed himself in epigrammatic terms of the most uncomplimentary nature.

Colonel Corkhill lost his temper, and desired the Court to restrain the prisoner. Then said Guiteau: "You go slow, Corkhill; you are spotted, and as soon as this business is over the President will remove you."

In the cross-examination, Mr. Scoville began to show the wear and tear his brain had been subjected to during the trial, for the first time losing his temper and speaking angrily to the witness, Guiteau, whom nobody could restrain, jumped headlong into the argument, and the scene for a time was very exciting.

George W. Plummer was called. Guiteau immediately shouted: "I owe this man $20, and it has cost the Government $200 to get him here. I think the President's attention had better be called to the way you are squandering the Government's money, Corkhill; he might bounce you at once. You'll cost the Government two or three hundred thousand dollars at this rate."

Witness said he allowed the prisoner to occupy a desk in his law office in Chicago for several months. The prisoner moved out and took his, witness', desk with him. Witness went after it, and prisoner paid him for it. The prisoner seemed to have a good deal of collection business, and went in and out like any busy man.

Guiteau continually interrupted, and finally the witness said to him:

"It seems that your close relations with the Deity of late have corrupted your manners."

Witness never saw any signs of insanity in the prisoner; on the contrary considered him rather a bright fellow. Did not think his *Inter-Ocean* scheme a very crazy one. Had the men the prisoner mentioned taken hold of it, they would have made it successful. There were a good many wild schemes started in Chicago, and frequently men without money controlled those with money. Witness advised the prisoner to stick to the law and let theology alone. The prisoner said the law business was dull and he thought there would be more money in theology.

Guiteau—You are wrong there. I never went into theology to make money.

On cross-examination witness was asked why he should express surprise at a lawyer's taking up theology, and replied:

"Because there are several steps between the law and the ministry, and one does not usually jump from one to the other."

Grenville B. Hames, Judge of the Marine Court, N. Y., said he let the prisoner have desk room in his office for about eight months. He never detected any signs of insanity in him; he met him but casually, to be sure, but always found him polite and gentlemanly.

Stephen English, editor and proprietor of the *Insurance Times*, took the stand. Guiteau, interrupting, called out: "This man was in Ludlow Street Jail, and I got him out for $300."

Witness gave the circumstances under which he became acquainted with the prisoner. He was in jail under $40,000 bonds, charged with libel, and the prisoner acted as his attorney.

Guiteau frequently and noisily interrupted the witness, calling him a liar and a perjurer, and at one time shouted: "There isn't an insurance company in New York that don't know what a fraud you are."

Mr. McLean Shaw, a lawyer of New York City, followed on behalf of the prosecution.

"Ah!" exclaimed the prisoner, "I am glad to see you, Mr. Shaw. You are a good fellow. I rented an office from you and you lent me $50." [Laughter.] Witness stated that Guiteau rented an office from him in 1871. He considered him perfectly sane in 1873. Witness did not approve of prisoner's manner of doing business, and requested that he would get an office elsewhere. Witness further stated that he always regarded the prisoner as a vain, egotistical man with a craving for notoriety.

"This is false!" exclaimed Guiteau; "I never craved notoriety. This witness loves money so well that his judgment is warped against me."

Witness next stated that on one occasion Guiteau said to him that the world owed him a living, and he intended to have it. "I am bound," said the prisoner at this conversation, "to be notorious before I die; and if I can't get notoriety in any other way, I will shoot one of our prominent men."

This statement caused a sensation in court.

Guiteau got up wildly, and, pounding on the desk, declared that he never said anything of the sort. Mr. Scoville entered an exception to this description of evidence.

"What else," asked Mr. Corkhill, "did the prisoner say in this connection?"

"Well," answered the witness, "he said 'I will imitate Wilkes Booth if necessary.' I suggested that he might get hung, and he remarked, 'Well, that is an after consideration; I will get notoriety, anyway.'"

Prisoner again became furiously excited. Pounding the table with his clenched fist, he bawled to the witness:

"You are a low, dirty, stinking liar! Your statement is false from beginning to end. You profess to be a churchman, but I will publish you to the world as a liar. When you go back to New York you will be the laughing stock of your friends, if you have any."

"When did this conversation occur?" asked Mr. Scoville, in the cross-examination.

"I can't fix the date," answered the witness; "but it was in my office some time in 1872."

"No; of course you can't fix the date, you miserable liar," again broke out the prisoner.

Other questions were propounded to the witness, who, however, persisted in the statement that the prisoner told him about this desire for notoriety and his determination, if necessary, to secure it as stated before.

The prisoner could not contain himself during this evidence. He saw the impression it made on the audience, and tried to counteract its effect by denouncing the witness. The Court, counsel, and Mrs. Scoville tried to appease his furious rage, but he kept on exclaiming at every break in the witness' statement that he was a miserable, contemptible liar.

Witness, when at last he got a chance to reply to Mr. Scoville, said the conversation was probably one cause why he requested the prisoner to look for another office. Other reasons were that he did not pay his rent, and clients came around charging that he defrauded them out of money.

He had mentioned this conversation to several friends, one of whom might have told the prosecution of it.

Prisoner (interrupting again)—"Then you kept your mouth shut for eight years? You are a colossal liar."

Mr. Scoville—"Did this conversation ever recur to your mind until after President Garfield was shot?"

"I don't know," replied the witness; "perhaps I would never have recalled it if the prisoner had not shot President Garfield."

This evidence was attentively listened to, and the prisoner's squirming antics during its delivery were one of the curiosities of the case.

Our readers will notice that we at times go back to the testimony given during the preceding week. This will be found to be a great help in getting at the best points of the case.

Despite the fact that the temperature of the court room was disagreeably near the freezing point, the court room was crowded to its utmost capacity, on the morning of December 31st, long before Guiteau was brought in. The prisoner took his seat in the dock without removing the heavy overcoat in which he was muffled, and complacently surveyed the audience. He proceeded to justify his reputation as the "man who never knowingly made a joke in his life" by calling out, "One of my guards, Mr. Cunningham, has got an eleven pound baby for a New Year's present." [Laughter, in which the jury heartily joined.]

Dr. Gray took the stand and gave the greater part of the conversation between himself and the prisoner in the jail. Guiteau interrupted him, saying, "That don't correspond with your evidence, Doctor. You went into inspiration in the other part of it."

Mr. Scoville objected to the statement of witness, "he said nothing of inspiration or divine pressure," and urged that witness must give the conversation, or the substance of it, as it occurred; that it would be the province of the jury to say what should be inferred from it. Witness qualified the statement by adding: "I asked him questions, and my statement is based upon his replies."

Witness continuing, said: "The prisoner used the expression, 'When I made up my mind.'"

Guiteau shouted: "Making up my mind was the result of the grinding pressure. That's where the inspiration comes in. Please get that straight while you are about it."

Mr. Scoville again objected that the witness was losing sight of the question and going into an argument.

Guiteau—"He's forgotten what he testified to. Corkhill must have gotten hold of him and instructed him what to say to-day. That's what is the matter with him."

Mr. Scoville disclaimed any desire to interrupt the witness, but the prosecution held him to the strict requirement that he should make his objections specifically, and he must therefore stop the witness at every point where he was satisfied an objection would lie.

Guiteau continually interjected comments, and, with Mr. Scoville's frequent objections, the witness soon became sensibly disturbed, and when asked to go on said: "There has been so many interruptions I don't know where I am."

Guiteau quickly retorted—"I should not think you do, nor any one else. I have been trying all the morning to find out where you are. The fact is you're badly lost this morning, Doctor. We'll have to send a small boy to find you."

The witness was about to state some reason which induced him (witness) to form the opinion that the prisoner was sane at the time he visited him at the jail, when Guiteau again interrupted him and called out, "Doctor Gray is devoting himself to an argument to the jury this morning, which he has no right to do. He should confine himself to facts. Porter will take up the arguments—(sarcastically), Judge Porter, I mean."

Mr. Scoville objected that the witness was volunteering an argument instead of adhering to a statement of facts.

Witness, with some feeling, replied, "I am under oath, Mr. Scoville, and I do not care to volunteer anything which is not strictly and appropriately evidence in this case."

Guiteau—"Then you had better stop talking if you don't want to volunteer anything."

Witness had seen a number of cases where persons laboring under insane delusions had committed acts of violence and had afterwards recovered their sanity, but did not recall an instance of recovery within a shorter period than three months. This reply was corroborative of previous testimony, and strongly opposed to the prisoner's claim that he recovered instantly from the "irresistible pressure" (or insane delusion) after he had shot the President.

Witness was asked to give his opinion on "hereditary," and replied, "it is the transmission of physical likeness and similitude. It is the rule in physical characteristics, but in transmission of susceptibility to disease it is the exception. An accident is not the rule."

Witness had never heard the word "pressure" used in connection with an insane case other than in a physical sense; he presumed it might be used to indicate strength of feeling. He did not think a man acting under divine pressure who should commit a homicide would be apt to appeal to the law and the civil authorities for protection for the consequences of his act.

Witness did not find a single circumstance as narrated by the prisoner that would indicate to his (witness') mind insanity. He was of opinion, judging by his examination of the prisoner in jail, and from his observation of him in court, that he is sane at this time.

Colonel Corkhill then read to the witness, with an apparent view of its vivisection, the hypothetical question of the defence, and, turning to Mr. Scoville, said: "You see, Mr. Scoville, I have submitted your own question."

Mr. Scoville—"Yes; only you don't read it with the same emphasis you do your own."

Col. Corkhill—"Precisely so; because I don't believe in it as I do in mine."

Witness replied: "I would not like to answer that hypothetical question because it evidently means to apply to the prisoner, and I could not answer it, if referring to him, knowing what I do of him from my own observation and examination. I could not answer it as a hypothetical case, because, in my judgment, it does not describe an insane state."

Witness then analyzed the question clause by clause, and severely criticized it.

Colonel Corkhill then read the lengthy hypothetical questions of the prosecution.

Guiteau suggested that there was no necessity to repeat "that bosh," as everybody had heard it a dozen times. The suggestion was unheeded, and the prisoner added, "Two-thirds of that is false, and it makes me mad every time I hear it read."

As the reading proceeded he continually called out: "That's false." "All false." "How do you know?" "That's Smith's lie," and similar expressions.

Witness replied: "I believe him to have been sane on July 2d."

Guiteau shouted: "The whole substratum of this thing is false. How can the Doctor give a truthful answer?"

Feigning in Court.

Witness then gave at great length and in full details what he had observed in the conduct and sayings of the prisoner in court that led him (witness) to believe in his sanity. Referring to the prisoner's claim that the Deity inspired the act, he was interrupted by Guiteau, who called, "Yes, and He'll take care of it, too, Dr. Gray. I'll stake my life on it."

Witness was asked: "Do you think the prisoner has been feigning in court?" and replied: "Yes, I do. He claims an inspiration from the Deity. I do not believe that he believes any such thing, and in such a sense he is feigning and acting a part."

Guiteau—"No such thing; I never feign. You are paid for your opinion; the jury is not."

Mr. Scoville began the cross-examination. Witness was asked if he had testified as an expert in cases of persons on trial for capital crime, but before he could reply, Guiteau supplemented the question by calling out: "How many men have you helped to hang, Doctor?"

Witness was not aware of a case where he had pronounced a sane man insane, or where he had adjudged an insane man sane. He admitted, however, that his views upon some types of insanity had changed since he began to study on the subject.

Guiteau—"You live to learn, then, like other people. If you live twenty years longer you may know something about insanity. You may reach the Abrahamic type by that time. You are a growing man, Doctor."

Witness stated that he abandoned the theory of "moral insanity" as far back as 1854. He did not think it would be found in his reports subsequent to that date as a distinct classification. After some further questions on this subject, Guiteau broke out impatiently: "The amount of it is these experts will swear to anything for money. They will swear to things to-day they would not have thought of swearing to twenty-five years ago, or would swear to twenty-five years hence. This subject of insanity is a progressive one."

Witness was asked how he came to visit Washington to testify in this case, and replied, "I did not care to come, but the president of the Board said he thought it my duty to come."

Mr. Scoville—"Then you came on his interpretation of your duty."

Witness (indignantly)—"No, sir, I came on a telegram."

Guiteau added, "How about Corkhill's money? I guess that was the influence that brought you here. This fellow Corkhill has got a bunghole in the Treasury that will run out $100,000 before he gets through with this case. It's about time President Arthur was attending to his case. I wouldn't let him stay here a week if I was President. However I'll attend to Corkhill in '84."

A recess was then taken.

After recess the cross-examination progressed without incident for half an hour. Mr. Scoville endeavored to force an acknowledgment from the witness that the conversations and conduct of the patient were the chief means of determining his sanity or insanity.

Witness insisted it was only an incident, not the essential element in the determination.

Mr. Scoville—"Why, you don't have any other means when they are alive, do you? You can't get at the brain to examine it, can you?"

Witness—"Well, we don't kill them especially for the purpose of examining their brains."

Mr. Scoville—"Well, I don't know what you scientists might do or claim that you could do."

Guiteau—"The experts on this case want to kill the man and then examine his brain afterwards."

Witness said he had seen some forty cases of feigned insanity. He was asked if he had ever seen any case of feigned insanity that resembled that of the prisoner (assuming that he is feigning), and replied: "I have not seen any insanity, real or feigned."

Being asked to explain, he added he meant to say in respect of his assertions that he is feigning.

Mr. Scoville—Then you mean to say the prisoner had told a lie in regard to the inspiration theory.

Witness repeated his answer in the same terms and declined to give a categorical answer without qualification.

Finally the hour of adjournment arrived. Guiteau, who had been listlessly following the proceedings, called out: "To-morrow will be New Year, 1882. I shall receive to-morrow in jail, and shall be happy to see all who succeed in getting in. I wish every one a happy New Year. Come, Scoville, it's three o'clock, let's go home."

As we have elsewhere stated in this book it is our intention to give the reader a comprehensive account of this great trial, and to follow with more minute details. The character of Guiteau is thus more fully shown and will stand out more clearly, and our history of the case prove more interesting.

The farcial trial of Guiteau was continued during that week with more "side-splitting" antics and interpolations than ever on the part of the impish assassin. The business of the week was, on the part of the defence, to prove insanity, and on the part of the prosecution, to rebut. Dr. Spitzka, an expert, was a witness for Guiteau and declared him insane, with many physiological reasons added to the measurements of the villain's cranium, and of the fact that one side of his head is smaller than the other. This, though several hatters were at hand to rebut by evidence that all men's heads are larger on one side than on the other. To this counsel suggested that "mad as a hatter" was an old time saying which, now for the first time, was likely to be an officially proven fact. When Gen. J. S. Reynolds was recalled and examined the "fun was fast and furious."

The witness said, in response to a question by the District Attorney, that besides the personal motive of curiosity, his reason for visiting the jail was to ascertain whether there was any socialistic plot in the assassination, and he was satisfied that there was not, and that Guiteau had no associate.

"That is entirely too thin," said the prisoner. "You went there as the special agent of the government. What is the use in lying about it?"

Mr. Scoville looked over the memoranda from which the witness read, and discovered parts that had not been read, as for instance, a declaration by the prisoner that he could rank with Conkling, Logan and other Republican leaders.

"I never said," exclaimed the prisoner, "that I could rank with them; but as a matter of fact, I think I could."

The witness on being pressed by Mr. Scoville to state why he had made a memoranda of his visits to the jail if he had not expected to make use of them, replied that it was to give correct information to the Attorney General, and that after each interview he recited to the Attorney General and the District Attorney what had occurred, using his memoranda for the purpose.

The District Attorney then read newspaper extracts which Reynolds took to the jail and read to the prisoner. They comprised telegraphic despatches from Senator Conkling, expressing abhorrence of the prisoner's act; also reports of interviews with Fred Grant, Senator Logan and others; also editorials on the assassination. The reading of them by the District Attorney was interrupted by exclamations from the prisoner like these:

"That is false. General Grant was always very kind and polite to me. He liked the ring of my speech."

"That is what Fred Grant says. He is a nice youth, is he not? He is too lazy to get a decent living. He is a dead beat—not I."

"I used to be a member of Beecher's church. He was supposed to be a virtuous man then, and perhaps he is now."

"I used to go up to Logan, pat him on the back, and say: 'How are you, General?' He thought I was a good fellow. Then they all turned against me, just as Peter did when he denied the Saviour when he was on the cross and in trouble. But they have got over it now, and they are coming up like proper men."

"My life would have been snuffed out at the depot that morning if God Almighty had not protected me. I was thinking about it this morning when I awoke and it seemed to me that that was the most audacious thing a man could do to shoot down the President surrounded by Cabinet officers and the police. I would not do it again for a million dollars. But I was in such a desperate state of mind under the pressure upon me that I could not have resisted it if I were to be shot down the next moment. My free agency was destroyed."

In reference to another newspaper extract speaking of Guiteau's boast that if he got the Austrian mission he would fill the position with proper dignity, the prisoner cried out:

"That part is true." [Laughter.]

Mrs. Ellen C. Grant, of Fourteenth street, Washington, was the next witness. As she took the stand the prisoner said:

"Mrs. Grant is a very fine lady and keeps a first-class boarding-house. I owe her $47. I will pay you very shortly, Mrs. Grant. If the men do not respond that I called upon yesterday I will call their names right out in meeting."

The witness testified that the prisoner had boarded in her house forty-one days, leaving on the last day of June. The witness never noticed in the prisoner anything indicating unsoundness of mind. She had considered him as intelligent as anyone in her house. She noticed nothing peculiar about him.

When Mr. Scoville began to ask the witness as to her competency to form an opinion about insanity and whether she had expressed an opinion that the prisoner was insane, Guiteau broke out:

"Mrs. Grant is close-mouthed like myself. There is no use in quizzing on cross-examination, Scoville. You are as stupid as a jackass this morning. You have not got brains enough for this business. Your place is in examining abstracts of title in Chicago. That is all you are fit for as a lawyer."

Mrs. Annie Dunmire, the prisoner's divorced wife, was then called to the stand. The prisoner denounced Corkhill for calling her.

"This lady," he exclaimed, "is married and has children, and it is an outrage for Corkhill to be permitted to take her and dig up her reputation, which I will have to do if she attempts to do me any harm. I ask the Court to stop this man Corkhill. He is an old hog. He has no character or conscience or sense and he is using his official position to traduce this lady. If I were President of the United States I would kick that man out of office in two hours. I want to make a speech to President Arthur. There are scores of first-class lawyers in New York city whom he knows, high-toned, Christian, conscientious men, any one of whom would be a hundred thousand times better than Corkhill. I ask President Arthur as a personal favor and in the name of the Republican party to kick this man out of office at once. I know Mr. Arthur and I have a right to make this personal request of him. If he is the man I take him for he will act on it at once."

The witness said she was married to

As developed during the trial, Guiteau starts a lecture in Boston, and leaves in disgust, because the audience was "too thin."

Enthüllung während des Prozesses. Guiteau will in Boston eine Vorlesung halten und geht voll Mißmuth Weg, weil das Auditorium nicht zahlreich genug war.

the prisoner on the 3d of July, 1869, in Chicago. After they moved to New York her husband followed law and politics. He was engaged in the Greeley campaign and expected as a reward to be appointed minister to Chili.

The district attorney asked the witness whether, in her association with the prisoner, she had ever noticed any insanity and her reply was, "I never did."

The district attorney, to Mr. Scoville —You may take the witness.

The Prisoner—Thank you, Mr. Corkhill; that is the decentest thing you have done on this trial. (Turning to Mr. Scoville)—Cut your cross-examination short, Scoville, and let us get to something else.

Mr. Scoville—Have you said since the 2d of July last that you considered the prisoner of unsound mind when you lived with him? A—No; I never have said so.

The Prisoner—What is the use of going into that, Scoville? You are a consummate jackass and I would rather have a ten-year-old boy to try this case than you. You have got no brains, no conception. You cannot see a foot ahead of you. Get off the case and I will do the business myself. I could have got three or four first-class lawyers to defend the case if you had not elbowed them out with your consummate egotism and vanity. You are taking altogether too much responsibility on yourself. I have got the heavy work myself to do before the Court and the jury.

During the cross-examination of Dr. Allan McLane Hamilton, of New York, Guiteau interrupted and explained to the doctor and the Court what he (Guiteau) considered insanity. Said the prisoner:

"I will tell you what insanity is. It is an irresistible desire to do something that you cannot help doing. That is my definition of insanity. I do not care a snap about the shape of the head, or the way that the tongue hangs. When a spirit comes over you and overpowers you (pounding on the table by way of emphasis) that is insanity."

When Rev. Dr. J. L. Withrow, of Boston, was called, Guiteau at once called out:

"Dr. Withrow is the honored pastor of the Park street Church, Boston, where I used to attend church when I was there. He is a very fine gentleman."

The witness related an incident within his knowledge. Guiteau called upon him in 1879 and said he was from Chicago, where he had been a co-worker with Moody. Ingersoll had been lecturing and Guiteau asked to be allowed to deliver a lecture in his (witness') church in answer to Ingersoll. Witness declined to have the church used for that purpose, and Guiteau argued with great earnestness that Ingersoll was doing great injury among the young men, and should be answered. He thought that he (prisoner) could answer him. Witness observed him during the winter at the meetings and social gatherings of the church and never saw the least indication of unsoundness of mind; but, on the contrary, thought he possessed unusual shrewdness—correcting himself, witness added: "I should say cuteness."

Guiteau—What's the difference, Doctor?

Answer—The one means brighter than the other.

Colonel Corkhill—And of larger calibre.

Guiteau—He didn't say that, Corkhill. You must have slept well last night; that's the smartest thing you have said yet.

Upon cross-examination the witness was asked to give the general tone of the prisoner's remarks at the social meetings, and replied that the prisoner generally took part in the discussions upon whatever subject might be under discussion; that he was always critical and accusative, rather than conciliatory and kind.

Guiteau—I always spoke to the point, incisive and gritty; that's me. There is no nonsense or romance in my composition. If there had been I might have gone through the world more smoothly.

During the brief absence of a juror who was taken ill Guiteau made another speech. He said:

"It's very evident to the mind of every one that the sole object of this kind of examination is to show that I know the difference between right and wrong. That has nothing whatever to do with this case. The only question is whether or not my free moral agency was destroyed when I was impelled upon the President. That's the point, Judge, and it knocks the bottom out of your theory."

After a short pause he broke out again, and with increased vehemence:

"I'm not here to save my neck from the gallows; I'm here for vindication, for justice, and for right."

Judge Cox—"Well, that will do; now suspend your remarks."

Guiteau—"All right; when I get to the jury I'm going to talk to them on this subject. This is just a little incidental speech to put in the time."

The weight of testimony was conclusively against the prisoner during the week, but nevertheless he kept up his clowning and his Merry Andrew antics with grimaces and grins that could not conceal the desperation and terror which supported him in his acting—for acting it evidently was.

The divorced wife of the assassin and her husband visited him in his cell before leaving Washington for the West, and a remarkable leave-taking and interchange of good wishes occurred. Really this case brought out not only more "cranks" but more of the queerest specimens of humanity and the strangest codes of honor and morality from the remote corners of the land than the wildest opium dreamer could ever have imagined had an existence.

We shall now continue to give our readers an account of each week (after the style of the foregoing reading matter) up to the really important parts of the trial. Then we will give you the case in detail.

Guiteau's Head.

About this time many interesting features were the order of the day, but a new feature was the taking of a plaster cast of the assassin's head by Theodore Mills. The pampered villain was persuaded to shave off his beard in order that the full effect of his physiognomy might be given by the artist's work. At first he objected, but his vanity being touched by the assurance that his features would come out stronger without than with the beard he consented. The measurement of the assassin's head showed that the circumference was 23¼ inches, while a phrenological expert got his hand in among the mob of manipulators of the villain's head and detected that his "self-esteem" was 6½ inches and his "firmness" 6¼ inches. Mr. Mills said that in his examination of the prisoner he found the faculties on the left side of the head appeared to be normal and well developed, but the right side of the head was almost flat, as though depressed by a heavy weight. The front of the head was also found to be one inch shorter than behind, and take it for all in all, he says, the assassin's head is the most curiously shaped of any he has ever examined. Guiteau seemed to revel in the delightful contemplation that he had a top-sided head and that his faculties on one side seemed to be almost entirely lacking. He was more cranky than ever during the trial after this examination had been made, and made much fun for the mob by his arguments in favor of the theory of his own insanity and by quarreling with his brother-in-law and counsel, Mr. Scoville, occasionally even turning upon his sister and giving her a "dressing down" to the delight of all observers.

D. McLean Shaw, who had testified that in a talk he had with Guiteau the latter had said he would imitate Wilkes Booth, was recalled by Mr. Scoville. When the assassin saw him he said excitedly:

"This is the man who told the lie about Booth. We have your record, Shaw, over there in New Jersey, where you were indicted for perjury."

In answer to Scoville's questions, Shaw said he had been indicted and tried for alleged perjury in New Jersey, but had been acquitted. The assassin here burst out with:

"There is not a word of truth in this Booth story, and you know it! God Almighty will curse you for it. You are marked for life. It is not likely I would wait ten years to kill some great man. It's the most outrageous thing ever concocted by human being."

Guiteau never ceased his tirade till the end of the day's session, and as he was led out, he was still denouncing Shaw and hurling defiance and sarcasm at Corkhill.

The testimony of Dr. A. McLane Hamilton was to the effect that Guiteau is not afflicted with insanity, and was not so afflicted on the 2d of July when he committed the murder.

In a long cross-examination of the witness by Mr. Scoville touching the exercise of the will as related to insanity, Guiteau burst forth again in his most frantic style of oratory:

"The will is controlled by spirits—not by intellectual process. You had better drop this, gentlemen, and put Clark Mills on the stand. He is a better man for you. Dry that thing up." (Alluding to Dr. Hamilton, the witness.) "Clark Mills took a cast of my face. He thought that some one hereafter would be interested in it. He thought I was a great man. He was the man that did Jackson opposite the White House. He thinks I am a greater man than Jackson, though Jackson has been President and I haven't been President yet. Mills wants to immortalize his name by getting it on my bust, so I took off my beard for his benefit. He is a better man for you than this one. He said that one side of my head was badly deficient."

After the brazen assassin had gotten off this tirade the examination of the witness proceeded. Dr. Wilson being called, and a long hypothetical question being put to him, Guiteau burst out again with:

"Let me say right here that Corkhill has made a very clear outward statement of the transaction; but what does he know about the spiritual pressure on me? The act is a matter for the Lord and for this jury, and for the Court and me to pass upon. Here is this quartette—the Lord and the Court and the jury and me. That is a mere outward statement of the transaction. The spiritual causes forcing me to the act are entirely unstated."

Poor Scoville took the witness in hand for cross-examination, and this is the way his assassin brother-in-law "went for" him:

"You are as stupid, Scoville, as the witness is. You are just compromising my case every time on cross-examination. You are not fit to be on this case at all. If I had some first-class criminal lawyer, he would show you how to do this business. I would have got John D. Townsend, of New York, or Judge Magruder, of Maryland, if you had not shoved them off with your confounded vanity and egotism. You are no more fit to manage this case than a ten-year-old school-boy. You have no ability in examining witnesses. Your business is in examining titles. You had no business to come here at all and compromise me with your blunderbuss way."

Then he stopped. Scoville went on placidly asking a few questions, but soon Guiteau broke out worse than ever. Said he:

"It is an outrage on justice for this man to come here. He has had no experience in criminal matters, and he is compromising my case. I would rather take my chance, even at this late hour, with Charley Reed, who is a first-class criminal lawyer, than with this idiot, who is compromising my case all the time. He has no wit, no sense; and between Corkhill and him, I have a pretty hard time." [Laughter, which seemed to put the prisoner in better humor, and in which he joined.]

Mr. Scoville for the first time during the trial seemed to be annoyed, worried, and humiliated by the prisoner's speech. He had difficulty in repressing his emotion, as he said to the Court that he had to notice what the prisoner said, and that he should be very glad to have the assistance of Mr. Reed.

The prisoner seemed to relent a little as he noticed Mr. Scoville's emotion, and he said, encouragingly, "You are doing first-rate, Scoville; but make your cross-examination short. You hurt the case by your inexperience in cross-examination."

Scoville, try as he might, could not conceal his chagrin, and seemed "all broken up" mentally by the annoyance and ridicule of the situation. "What a wonder he does not throw the villain's case up and leave him to his fate!" was the general remark among the audience.

The next day after this row Guiteau addressed the Court, saying Scoville did not suit him as a criminal lawyer, and he wished consent of the Court to have Mr. Charles H. Reed assume the active duties of the case.

Mr. Reed thereupon took charge, but it made little difference, for Guiteau interrupted as often as usual. Mr. Davidge, of the prosecution, venturing in a few remarks, Guiteau silenced him with the remark: "Davidge, you have too much to say in this case. You are as bad as a man born with the diarrhœa."

And so the circus went on, the change of counsel making not the slightest abatement of the buffoon's merry antics.

The trial was now nearing its end, and had, by this time, been reduced to a dreary repetition of experts to the effect that Guiteau was not insane, but merely playing a part, and that, too, somewhat awkwardly.

The prisoner's conduct became so obstreperous that the Court lost all patience with him, and the counsel got into a general muss over him. Mr. Scoville said he was as anxious as any one that the assassin should be made to keep quiet. Guiteau retorted that he spoke because Scoville was a jackass in the case two-thirds of the time. Mr. Corkhill insisted that the prisoner should be placed in the dock. This was done, despite the assassin's whining that he might be shot by some one in the audience. For a few moments the prisoner was quiet; but when the plaster cast of his head was handed around he broke out again with a laugh, saying, "Why, it looks like Humpty Dumpty." Then he went on interrupting the witnesses, remarking, among other things, "There are two kinds of insanity, Corkhill—rank insanity and the Abrahamic style of insanity. I belong to the Abraham school." He suggested to the Court several times that the witnesses should simply tell what they knew about Abraham, then get their money and go home. The spectators of his antics were kept in roars of laughter.

Each day the prisoner alluded to the risk he ran of being shot. Said he, "The first thing you know some crank will be shooting at me. He will not hit me, but he is liable to hit some one else." A letter which Guiteau had written to Don Cameron, asking the loan of $500, but which was intercepted by Scoville, was presented to a witness for his judgment as to whether a man who could seriously write thus to a stranger was thoroughly sane.

Then the prisoner broke out again. Said he: "If my brother had presented the letter he would probably have got the money. But as he would not be decent but preferred to act in a mean, dirty way he did not get the money. Did you never borrow money, Scoville?"

Guiteau took offence at Scoville's pressing the witness with questions in regard to his sanity. He retorted at various points in the cross-examination, saying among other things, "If you had sent that letter, Scoville, to Senator Cameron you would have evidence that you were a crank. But you have got no standing with such men as Cameron. You do not know how to treat them. I was in friendly relations with Senator Cameron and there was nothing strange in my writing that letter. Anybody but a numbskull like Scoville would see it. I claim to be on perfectly friendly relations with Senator Cameron. I have met him and know him and he knows me. There is nothing inconsistent in my writing to him for money. If my brother had delivered the letter like a decent man I would have probably got the money. You had better get off the case, Scoville, and go back to Chicago. My brother, too, had better go back to Boston and try to get some money to pay his debts."

Dr. Walter Kempster, of Winnebago, Wis., superintendent of the Northern Hospital for the Insane, testified that he had examined the head of the prisoner and had thought that the deviations in it were more marked than were shown by the plaster cast. He was satisfied there was no shape of the head that indicated insanity. The witness showed to the jury diagrams of the heads of various persons who, he said, were all of prominence. Among them were the heads of Judge Carter, Chief Justice of the Supreme Court of the District of Columbia; Judge Wylie, Treasurer Gilfillen, Gov. Claflin, Robert G. Ingersoll, and District Attorney Corkhill. In pointing out the deviations in the various heads the witness said that Mr. Ingersoll's bulged out very much on one side.

"It bulges out on the wrong side, doesn't it?" suggested Mr. Davidge.

"It shows," said Guiteau, with an impish grin, "that Ingersoll and I are badly cracked." The witness continued: "Col. Corkhill's head has a very marked impression upon one side." The assassin burst into a laugh, saying, "I bet you could put your foot in the depression in his head."

Witness continued that the depression was very similar to that noticed in the prisoner's head. "Oh, he's cracked worse than I am," said Guiteau.

The trial during the week degenerated into a fierce wrangle between the opposing lawyers, who lost their tempers all around.

In the course of the quarrel Judge Porter protested against the course taken by Mr. Scoville in the cross-examination as, he said, it was a waste of valuable time.

This was the cue for Guiteau again. "You are getting tired of this case," said he. "So am I. I am tired, too. Suppose you withdraw the indictment and let us go home."

The proceedings in the trial of the assassin Guiteau, at Washington, on the following week were not so lively as heretofore, nor were the jokes and antics of the monster clown of the same "side-splitting" quality that the audience had found them during the show's long run. Guiteau, while as devilish and blasphemous as ever, seemed to play his part at times "with the soft pedal down." Perhaps he began to see the shadow of the great coming event of retributive justice.

The counsel for the prisoner made a strenuous effort to get in some additional evidence of experts as to Guiteau's insanity, past and present.

The defence as strenuously opposed the motion, and a sharp and bitter discussion arose among the lawyers.

Mr. Scoville alluded to the difficulty of getting witnesses for the defence, and said that it was only common justice that the prisoner should have a fair trial. The prosecution had, he said, the United States Treasury behind them, and it was wrong to crowd the defence when it was known that there was no money to recompense their witnesses except the ordinary fee.

Colonel Corkhill held that every fair opportunity had been allowed the defence.

Mr. Scoville eloquently contended that law and justice were now on the side of the defence, and that everything tending to show Guiteau's insanity should be admitted.

The prisoner listened attentively to the arguments of both sides. He made no interruption, but toyed with his eyeglasses and smiled at the ladies.

In reply, the District Attorney said there never was a case in the country where so much liberality had been extended to the defence.

Guiteau got excited, and said it was necessary that the state of his mind on the 2d of July should be presented to the jury.

The guards endeavored to keep him quiet but he shouted, "You keep quiet and let me alone, or I will slap your mouth. I am here as my own counsel."

Judge Cox rendered a long decision. He said that he appreciated the difficulties the defence had labored under, but did not see the necessity of allowing any testimony in the line indicated. The evidence now proposed was of vague and uncertain character, and did not strike him as being admissible.

The assassin broke in with a statement that one of the witnesses was an officer who took him to the jail after the assassination, and knew of his state of mind at the time.

The guards were unable to pacify him. He protested against every effort to keep him quiet. "If I had plenty of money," he cried, "I could get scores of people to swear that I was crazy as a loon on the 2d of July."

The Court rapped for order several times.

The prisoner became wroth and refused to keep still. One of the guards endeavored to pacify him.

"You shut up!" he shouted. "You cannot keep me still. How are you going to do it? I want to go home. I am tired of this business. Let us end this business."

James J. Brooks, Chief of the Secret Service of the Treasury Department, was then placed on the stand by the defence. He said he had several conversations with Guiteau shortly after the murder, and detailed the prisoner's remarks in relation to the tragedy. The statements did not vary from the other evidence on this point.

Mrs. Scoville cried aloud at this relation, and the prisoner said the circumstances had been stated correctly by the witness. When told of Garfield's precarious condition in one of these conversations Guiteau said, "Poor fellow, I'm sorry. I wish I had given him a third bullet and put him out of misery."

Here Guiteau again became restless, and had several altercations with the Deputy Marshal in charge of him. "Sit down and mind your business," he shouted. "You are nobody, and I speak to 50,000,000 of people. I know my rights, and you cannot keep me quiet. Sit down. I am happy because I have been true to God and the American people. Everything has gone on as I anticipated, and everybody is happy except a few miserable cranks whom I don't care anything about and would spit upon if they were present."

Mrs. Scoville wanted to put in a photograph of the prisoner to show his condition prior to the murder, but the prosecution objected, and there was another war of words between counsel.

All testimony was then pronounced in, and the Court adjourned to allow the defence to present their propositions of law.

One day, while Mr. Scoville was at work in his office, a man whom he did not know entered the room. He introduced himself, saying he had come on a business errand. He had, he added, a business proposition to make, and hoped that Mr. Scoville would then and there be ready to close with the offer.

"I have come," said the man, "to offer you $1,000 for the body of Guiteau."

Mr. Scoville was, of course, greatly astonished and at first he thought he might have a crank to deal with. The man, however, very speedily persuaded Mr. Scoville that he was no crank, but had made the offer in good faith, and was ready upon signing the proper papers to hand Mr. Scoville the cash. It was suggested that possibly Guiteau might escape the gallows. The man said he had thought of all that but felt so confident of Guiteau's conviction and hanging that he was ready to run the risk. He would pay Mr. Scoville $1,000 upon the contract to deliver to him the dead body of Guiteau, and would take the risk of Guiteau not being hanged. He was extremely anxious to close the bargain at once, and seemed somewhat relieved when he learned that Scoville had not otherwise disposed of the body, nor, in fact, had received any proposition for it.

This proposition was submitted to Guiteau, and seemed to impress him favorably. After reflecting a moment, he said:

"I think I ought to bring more than that. Perhaps some other fellow will offer $2,000. Then I can pay my debts, and if I get a new trial that miserable Corkhill can't bring on a lot of fellows just to swear how much I owe them."

The offer was finally accepted, the assassin chuckling over the trade, as he felt sure he was not to be hanged, and that the speculator in "stiffs" will lose his money.

And now we must go back to a very interesting day in this great trial—that of Tuesday January 3d—and which necessarily gives you, in some parts, a repetition of evidence. Dr. Gray's testimony as an expert must not be ignored. There were many experts on the stand but their experience generally reached the one grand point, "Was, or Is this man Insane?"

On this Tuesday morning of which we speak the temperature of the court room was a few degrees only above the freezing point, and jury, court officials and spectators sat shivering in overcoats and wraps, while the reporters, with benumbed fingers, labored at serious disadvantage. An old and dilapidated furnace, which would not be half large enough if new and in good condition, proved wholly insufficient for heating purposes, and added materially to the other discomforts of the court room. Counsel were somewhat tardy, and the Court did not convene until ten minutes past ten.

Guiteau made his opening speech as follows "I had a very happy New Year's yesterday and hope every body else did. I had lots of visitors, hightoned, middle-toned and low-toned. That takes them all in, I believe. They expressed their opinions freely, and none of them want me hung. They all, without dissent, express the opinion that I shall be acquitted."

Dr. Gray took the stand and Mr. Scoville resumed his cross-examination.

Witness had not, in giving his opinion —on direct examination—that the prisoner was sane—taken into account the evidence of the prisoner himself, but taking that element into account, his opinion would still be the same that the pris-

Likenesses of the jury in this great case.
Bild der Geschworenen in diesem großen Prozesse.

oner is sane and was sane on the 2d of July.

A hypothetical question was propounded by Mr. Scoville involving the killing of a woman by her husband without any apparent motive, and witness was asked: "Would that act be any indication of insanity?"

Answer. It would be a very extraordinary act. I should want to make an examination to see if it was from passion, or if the man was drunk, or—

"Had disease of the brain," supplied Guiteau. "You would have to find disease of the brain before you could call him insane. That shows just how much you experts know about it."

Witness was asked if he was familiar with the case of Lieutenant Sanborn, who was killed by Dr. Wright at Norfolk, Va., and replied: "Yes, sir I was sent by the President to make an examination and give an opinion on the case."

"How much did you get for it?" shouted Guiteau.

Witness was closely questioned as to how or by what physical examination insanity and disease of the brain could be detected.

Q. Have you ever had patients in your asylum who have recovered? A. Yes, sir, I have.

Q. Have you seen persons who have recovered in three months? A. Yes, sir, I have.

Mr. Scoville—And were they discharged? A. Yes, sir.

Mr. Scoville—Well, now, if you experts were to examine such a patient immediately upon his discharge, could you tell by any physical indications that he had been insane only three months previous.

Witness (hesitatingly)—No, sir, without a history of the case.

Mr. Scoville—I thought so.

Guiteau—Your idea, Doctor, that a man can't be insane unless his brain is diseased is rather frivolous. You don't agree with the Saviour. You ought to study up spiritology; then you would catch new ideas.

Witness did not believe in what is termed by some writers "emotional insanity" or "moral insanity." "Kleptomania" he considered simply thieving; "dipsomania," drunkenness and "pysomania," incendiarism. Their designations were simply convenient terms which had been invented to cover certain crimes.

"Insanity," said witness, "is never transmitted any more than cancer. I never knew any one to be born with a cancer. A susceptibility to insanity is undoubtedly transmitted from parents to children, but insanity does not necessarily follow, except from some profound physical disturbance."

The examination progressed with tedious detail. In the effort to extract something favorable to the defence, counsel renewed his attack upon the witness again and again, and each time was met with an evasive or qualified reply. Finally, Mr. Scoville, with some importance, inquired: "Can you tell me, Doctor, how many direct replies you have given me this morning?"

A. I don't know that I have given you any. I propose to answer precisely in my own way, Mr. Scoville. I am under oath, and I propose to give you all the information bearing upon the case in my possession, but I do not care to drag my personalities into it any more than is possible.

The prisoner meanwhile had observed a marked decorum, at intervals gazing out of the window, but most of the time he appeared to be busily engaged in writing his autograph upon cards which were handed up to him from the audience by the attendants.

Mr. Scoville desired to put in evi certain tabulated statements from nual reports of the witness. From it appeared that of the fifty-four cases of homicide by insane people, seven of them were by persons acting under the insane delusion of Divine authority for their acts. At the request of the District Attorney witness described briefly these cases, and added, "Each case was one of marked insanity independent of the homicidal act."

A recess was taken.

After recess Dr. Gray was asked a few more questions by Mr. Scoville, when the District Attorney announced the conclusion of the evidence on the part of the Government.

Sur-rebuttal for the Defence.

Mr. Scoville walked over to the dock and conferred with the prisoner a few minutes. After returning to his seat he said: "Your honor, I am taken somewhat by surprise by the action of the prosecution in not calling several witnesses whose names had been given in as witnesses for the prosecution. These gentlemen, being employés of the Government, were in position to know something of the mental condition of the prisoner about the time of the shooting of the President. I do not know what action in the matter the defence will wish to take, but I will inform the Court tomorrow morning."

Dr. Bowker, of Kansas City, was then called by Mr. Scoville.

Witness met Mrs. Dunmire at Leadville, Col., and conversed with her. She said she had entertained grave doubts as to the mental condition of Guiteau at the time she obtained her divorce, and thought at the time, perhaps, she had better defer the divorce proceedings and await some further developments in the mental condition of her husband.

Clark Mills, the sculptor, was called for the purpose of identifying the plaster cast of Guiteau's head. At the first question, "Did you make a cast of the prisoner's head?" Mr. Davidge objected to any reopening of the question of insanity such as would be involved by the identifying of the cast by this witness. The whole question of insanity had been gone over directly, and, in rebuttal, the prosecution had already submitted the genuineness of the cast, and that was all that could be asked by the defence.

After further arguments, the Court ruled against Mr. Scoville, and the witness was withdrawn.

The prisoner undertook to read a letter, as he claimed, from an old friend of President Garfield's, in Ohio, showing that public opinion was making in his favor.

Judge Cox ordered him to be silent.

Guiteau—It shows the state of public opinion outside this court room.

Judge Cox—Be silent. Public opinion has nothing to do with this case.

Guiteau—When I speak I speak to fifty million people; not to this little crowd in this little court room.

Marshal Henry (rising and moving towards the dock)—Keep quiet, sir.

Guiteau—I've got through, sir.

The marshal whispered some instructions to the bailiff sitting in the dock. A moment later the prisoner started upon another harangue, and the bailiff put his hand upon his shoulder and attempted to quiet him.

Guiteau snarled out, "Get away from me, or I'll slap you in the mouth."

With this outburst he subsided, however, and turned his attention to writing autographs.

John W. Guiteau was again put upon the stand, and questioned in relation to Guiteau's letter to Senator Don Cameron.

Mr. Davidge—I object, your honor, to any attempt to introduce what has a prima facie appearance of manufactured testimony.

Guiteau—And so do I.

After arguments upon the question, the Court again ruled against the defence, and this witness was withdrawn.

Mr. Scoville again brought up the question of introducing new witnesses, and arguments were made pro and con. Agreement was finally made that the defence should submit in writing their motion, giving the names of witnesses and the facts to be testified to and supported by affidavit giving the reason why such witnesses were not introduced before.

There was an immense crowd about the City Hall at Washington, D. C., on the morning of January 12th, 1882. It was a more sensational gathering than had been witnessed for many a day. So tightly jammed and packed was the mob of men and women that to move about seemed absolutely impossible, save for those on the outer edges. The energies of Marshal Henry and his deputy, supported by the corps of bailiffs, were taxed to the utmost to handle and control the immense assemblage, and they were called upon to exercise the utmost patience in the performance of their duties. The men they could control, but the females gave them considerable trouble. They would not heed the announcement that the space was exhausted and further admission impossible, but pushed forward, trying to effect an entrance, and presumed upon the privilege of their sex to accomplish it. So persistent did they become that the officers of the court had to appear almost rude in compelling them to submit to their orders.

Messrs. Scoville and Reed arrived early, and soon behind them came Mr. Davidge, who was to lead off in the argument to the jury in behalf of the Government. He proceeded immediately to collect his papers and put them in shape for ready service when required. The remaining counsel for the Government entered the room with Judge Cox, pausing long enough to permit the jury to precede them. The assassin came last, as usual, and went to the dock, receiving from Mr. Scoville several letters as he passed the counsel table, which he began reading as soon as he got seated. Rossi, the great Italian tragedian, sat at the table of the prosecution during the morning. After recess the place that Rossi had occupied was filled by Stuart Robson, the well known American actor. Mr. Crane, the English actor, sat a little distance from the prosecution table. Rossi appeared much interested in Mr. Davidge's address, and congratulated that gentleman before leaving the court. Mr. Davidge's well modulated voice and pleasing cadences fell most agreeably upon the refined ears of the actor. When Mr. Davidge quoted with fine effect Macbeth's utterances when making his way to the chamber of Duncan, the actor's sympathy with the speaker was so strong that at every pause in the eloquent lines of the poet he nodded his head in approval.

At the close of the day a most sensational scene occurred. The District Attorney made a most violent speech against the assassin being allowed to again address the Court from the counsel table, as was proposed in his closing argument in his own defence. This set the prisoner off in a clamor, Mrs. Scoville into tears and loud sobs, and the audience into applause. For several moments the scene was very sensational and thrilling.

THE PROSECUTION'S OPENING.

Points Made by Mr. Davidge in His Address to the Jury.

As soon as Judge Cox took his seat on the bench Mr. Davidge began the opening speech for the prosecution. There was but a single point for discussion, he said, and that was the subject of insanity. The law did not contemplate that any man should coldly, deliberately and treacherously slay another and then say he had no malice. It was laid down plainly that a man shall not be protected against punishment if he knew what he was doing and that it was contrary to law unless the illegality and wrongfulness of the act was obliterated by mental disease. No disease of his moral nature would constitute any excuse, no belief, however profound; although a man, through reason and reflection, may reach the conclusion that an act is suggestive of a command of Almighty, it did not afford any excuse whatever for the perpetration of crime. This crime was more than murder, it was the murder of the head of the nation. It was said there was a divinity that hedged a king. We have no king, but one would suppose that the ruler of a republic such as ours would inspire respect equal to that inspired by any king or emperor. After paying a glowing tribute to the virtues and abilities of the late President he turned to the prisoner and sketched his character in scathing terms. "To sum up the character of this vile wretch," counsel said, "he had the daring of the vulture combined with the heart of a wolf."

The Assassin's Interruptions.

The speaker then detailed the circumstances preceding the assassin's conception of the crime, and as he gradually reached the conviction that "but one little life interposed between himself and possibly great benefits," Guiteau became restless, and for the first time since the opening of the court indicated, by his nervous twisting about, the preliminaries of a series of interruptions, which in this instance quickly followed. He denied Mr. Davidge's assertions, said his ideas came from the Lord, and told the counsel if he prayed more he would be a better man. As the horrible preparations for his crime were clearly and calmly related to the jury, Guiteau interrupted in his usual Billingsgate fashion. At one time, when his borrowing habits were alluded to, he cried: "How many due bills have you got out, Davidge?" At another: "I was in the Lord's hands, and am still. I will be protected." He listened attentively and was ready with a vulgar remark at every telling point. Instead of laughing at the fellow's impudent conduct the audience for once looked annoyed and angered.

Points Made by Mr. Davidge.

After recess Mr. Davidge took up the subject of inspiration and dwelt upon it at length, saying it was almost a mockery to argue upon such a claim. The evidence adduced by the defence in the effort to show insanity in the Guiteau family was also reviewed, the case of each member of the family being taken up in order. Then the counsel passed in review before the jury the habits of life and history of the prisoner from his birth up. His connection with the Oneida Community was dwelt upon, causing Guiteau to angrily interrupt the speaker every minute and to deny what was asserted. Once, when mentioning the testimony of Mr. Reed, the prisoner exclaimed:

"You'd better look out; Reed is going to speak to-morrow and he may tear you to pieces. He's had lots of experience in Chicago handling such fellows as you are and he's sent some of them to State Prison."

When Mr. Davidge reached Guiteau's career in Boston he caused a ripple of laughter by saying: "There is in Boston, among other things—and you must know all things are in Boston—a temple or building erected by the disciples or believers in the doctrine of Tom Paine, the atheist. I think the prisoner's peculiar conduct there when he lectured may be attributed to the fact that the company were out of accord with him and their ridicule angered and disgusted him."

The hour of 3 o'clock having arrived, Judge Porter suggested an adjournment, which was assented to by counsel for the defence. An exciting discussion then ensued upon Judge Cox inquiring if counsel desired to say anything upon Guiteau's request to be heard. "I want," shouted Guiteau, "to make the closing speech. I wouldn't trust the conclusion in my case to the best lawyer in America." The District Attorney, in a ringing speech, protested against Guiteau's being again allowed to take a seat at the counsel table. Applause from the audience, with the shouts of Guiteau and cries of "Order" from the bailiff, made an exciting scene for some minutes.

Guiteau was finally heard shouting through the din, "The American people will read my speech, and they are greater than this Court. The American people are trying this case. If you undertake to put on the gag law the court in banc will right me. My speech will make eight columns in the *Herald* and it reads like an oration of Cicero. It will go thundering down the ages, and don't you forget it; and as for you, Corkhill, President Arthur will soon dispose of you."

Mrs. Scoville was deeply affected and wept hysterically. Judge Cox finally told Mr. Scoville to read over the prisoner's speech and let the Court know if there was anything in it he desired to go before the jury. Without stating whether he would permit the prisoner to speak or not Judge Cox ordered an adjournment.

The next day the rain and slush had no terrors for those who had secured tickets to the trial. At an early hour the court room was crowded and at 10 o'clock possibly two hundred persons were patiently waiting upon the outside. Just before the opening of the court Deputy Marshal Williams announced that by order of the Court any demonstrations of applause on the part of the audience would be followed by the arrest and perhaps imprisonment of the offender. This was accompanied with the request that no one would attempt to leave the court room until recess. Mr. Davidge was early in his seat, and replying to an inquiry stated that he would speak on that day two hours and probably more. "That means all day," was suggested, and to this Mr. Davidge smiled, leaving the inference, if any, that such might be the case.

Upon the opening of the court Guiteau said: "In justice to myself and Mr. Davidge, I desire to say that I received a letter yesterday severely denouncing Mr. Davidge, and my remarks against him were based upon that. I have found out, however, that I was mistaken, and that Mr. Davidge is a high-toned Christian gentleman and a sound lawyer. I desire, therefore, to withdraw anything I said against him. I still entertain the same opinion of Corkhill, however. I'm satisfied I was wrong about Davidge, but right on Corkhill."

Mr. Davidge resumed his argument and review of the evidence. He showed up, by the evidence of J. W. Guiteau and other witnesses for the defence, the fallacy and absurdity of Mr. Scoville's pet theory that the prisoner was an imbecile.

Soon after the opening of the court Speaker Keifer and ex-Attorney General Taft entered and took seats on the bench.

After his opening speech Guiteau remained a quiet listener for an hour. Mr. Davidge having used some pretty strong language in alluding to Guiteau, such as "this unspeakable liar," the prisoner retorted, "Oh, you are making all that fine talk for money," following it up with frequent comments, "That happens to be false," "That isn't true," and similar expressions.

Mr. Davidge passed to the examination of the prisoner himself, his appearance upon the stand, what he had said and what capacity of intellect he had shown, proving conclusively that what had gone before had all been a sham and a hollow fraud. Mr. Scoville had dilated upon his morality and had asserted that lack of intellect was his failing. On the contrary he had shown upon the stand a wonderful memory, logic, reason and intellectual ability. Likewise, as the defence had claimed for virtue and morality, the prosecution had availed themselves of their right to show the contrary, and what had been the result? He had been shown to be such a monster of corruption, deceit, depravity and wickedness that the country looked on with a shudder.

"That might have been the case," shouted Guiteau, "in July, but it isn't the case now. If you could see some of the letters I have been receiving you would see that a good many people think I am one of the best and greatest men in the country."

Continuing, Mr. Davidge skilfully and with wonderful effect reviewed that portion of the testimony bearing upon the prisoner's moral character as evidenced in his past life. "All this time," said counsel, "no one accused him of insanity. In the estimation of his friends and his family he was sane enough for all the transactions of life, but, when his hand is red with blood and the outraged law claims him as a sacrifice on the altar of justice, we first hear of insanity."

Alluding to Guiteau's schemes in relation to the *Inter-Ocean*, Mr. Davidge said: We have to deal here with the plans of an audacious mind, but there is nothing in such a scheme to indicate insanity. It is a fact, I understand, that the stock of that paper, once worth $75,000, is now worth $1,000,000, and it was by putting into successful operation plans first suggested by the prisoner.

"Yes," shouted Guiteau, "the paper never was anything until I put some brains into it, and they have been running ever since on my brains."

Summing up this incident, Mr. Davidge said: "It was no indication of insanity; it was simply in keeping with his idea that the great moving brain and the one central figure of the day was that of Charles J. Guiteau."

"Thank you, Mr. Davidge," (sarcastically) called out the prisoner; "I'm glad you are beginning to think so. A great many other people think I'm the greatest man of the day, but I don't care a snap what they think. I haven't got a bit of egotism."

Mr. Davidge alluded briefly to the testimony of Mrs. Dunmire, the divorced wife of the prisoner. "The prosecution were debarred from entering upon those confidences which exist between husband and wife. The defence could have done so, but they did not. Mrs. Dunmire did not hesitate," said Mr. Davidge, " to testify emphatically that he was a sane man." "She don't know anything about me," called out Guiteau. "I haven't seen her for eight years."

Mrs. Scoville, who had been busily writing all the morning, shook her head angrily and ejaculated, "She's a liar, any way."

Her brother whispered a warning, but she repeated the comment still more emphatically.

Commenting upon the testimony of Dr. Spitzka, Mr. Davidge said: "Notwithstanding some of his remarkable statements, Spitzka never denied the prisoner's legal responsibility. Accepting all his evidence, even Spitzka brought the prisoner within the reach of the law and punishment."

After recess, Mr. Davidge resumed his argument with a review and discussion of the expert testimony.

Never before, he said, had so many men of eminence appeared upon a trial of this character. The treasury had been opened to secure the attendance of witnesses. More than twenty experts had been summoned for the defence, many of them men whose names were known in every household. They came here, they watched the prisoner, they listened to his evidence, and what was the result? With two exceptions they vanished from before the light of evidence like a cloud before the wind, and not one of them could come upon the stand and swear that this man was legally insane. They met and compared notes, and they could not testify other than to his sanity, with the exception of the two moral insanity men, and I regret to say it, neither of them would or could admit that they believed in a God. They vanished from before you and were permitted by the defence to withdraw without testifying.

Now what has been the result of all this evidence? This alleged fool has grown before you to a man of more than ordinary intellect. We have uncovered his moral nature. We have shown him to be in religion a hypocrite, at law a pettifogger, in all things a swindler; a denizen of jails, and a depraved and wicked wretch.

In answer to the prisoner's claim of Divine inspiration, Mr. Davidge read, with impressive effect, from the first chapter of the Epistle of James, 13th to 15th verses, inclusive.

The air of the room was very oppressive after the recess, and quite a ripple of excitement was caused by a sudden stir among the audience in the rear of the room, a lady having fainted. Judge Davidge suspended his remarks until the confusion should subside. The lady was removed from the court room.

Guiteau called out, "I think the most sensible thing to do, Your Honor, would be to let in a little fresh air."

This suggestion was immediately acted upon; the victim of insufficient oxygen was taken out, and Mr. Davidge resumed his speech.

In a few minutes Guiteau interrupted, sneeringly, "You're putting it all wrong, Davidge. You are talking for money now."

Without noticing the interruption, Mr. Davidge adverted to the period of two weeks, when, as he said, "the prisoner was making up his mind to commit the act."

"I was praying to find out the Lord's will," broke in the prisoner.

Mr. Davidge (partially turning to the Judge)—"Let him go on. I will hang him upon his own testimony;" a prediction, however, which appeared to have no terrors for Guiteau, for his interruptions became more and more frequent.

Allusion being made to his not paying his debts, he shouted: "I'm a better man than Corkhill in that particular. I always pay my debts when I have money. He don't pay his when he has money in his pocket."

Reading from the evidence Mr. Davidge quoted from Guiteau's own testimony this sentence:

"I don't tell my business to everybody; I keep my mouth shut."

Guiteau retorted: "That's true except here. I have to open it pretty often here," and in a few minutes he shouted in loud tones: Confer not with flesh and blood. That was Paul's idea, and that's mine. I get my advice from the Deity, not from flesh and blood. That's the way Paul got his work in, and that's the way I did mine. The trouble with you is, Davidge, that you don't know anything about the Deity. He knows about you, though, and you'll know something about him when he gets you down below."

Exciting scene.—Jones, in the role of an avenger, fires into the prison-van at Guiteau.

Aufregende Scene.—Jones welcher den Rächer spielt feuert einen Schuß auf Guiteau im Gefangenen-Wagen ab.

After disposing of the insanity and inspiration theories, Mr. Davidge continued: "There is not an element in this case that removes it from the category so carefully provided against in the courts. Here was a daring, audacious boy, who, in the Oneida Community, gave way to a life of lawless vice; later as a man, a theocrat who would overturn all law and churches; later, when he boasted himself to be of the firm of Jesus Christ & Co. You see the legitimate outcome of his wicked egotism. And it is just as legitimate and logical to find the true explanation of this crime in the same traits of inordinate vanity, desire of notoriety and reckless egotism. As I conceive, the true and only theory of his crime is this: He conceived the idea of this monstrous crime, believing that others were as wicked as himself, and those who would be benefited by it would in some way, interpose to save him from the damning consequences of his most heinous crime.

Guiteau continually interrupted with a constantly increasing exhibition of ugly temper. "You'll get the Deity down on you for the way you are conducting this case," he shouted, "and he'll eternally damn you, Davidge." Again he cried out, "the Attoney General refused to have anything to do with the case because he is a Christian gentleman, and he knew the Deity was on my side."

His interruptions became so noisy that Mr. Davidge paused for a moment, and said, "I trust, gentlemen, you will not draw any inference from the fact that I do not take occasion to reply to any of these falsehoods (turning his head toward the prisoner) that are being uttered here."

"You tell the truth and I'll let you alone," snarled the prisoner.

Mr. Davidge read in detail the evidence of General Reynolds, during which he was continually interrupted by the prisoner, and concluded his remarks with these words: "I promised you, gentlemen, that I would not make a set speech, and in closing I shall indulge in no peroration except to say to you that your countrymen and all Christendom are waiting for your verdict. I thank you, gentlemen, for your attention."

Guiteau added: "And I thank you, Mr. Davidge, for your speech. It is a very light one. I hope Porter will give us as light a one, too. He had better see President Arthur before he commences. I wrote the President about this matter a day or two ago."

On Saturday January 14th the court room was densely crowded in anticipation of the opening argument for the defence. At ten o'clock the prisoner was brought in and as soon as he had taken his seat, he opened the day's proceedings with the following speech:

"I received thirty checks yesterday, representing about $15,000; some of them are worthless and many of them are no doubt good; I don't want any one to send me a worthless check. I do my own banking business and my checks should be made out to my order. Any one who desires to send me money can do so, but I don't want any worthless checks."

Mr. Reed took a position immediately in front of the jury awaiting a signal from the Court to begin the opening argument for the defence.

All eyes were turned in that direction, when Mr. Scoville arose and addressed the Court, stating that he desired to know whether the prisoner would be allowed to speak in his own defence. If the Court proposed to accord him that privilege, both he (Mr. Scoville) and his associate (Mr. Reed) would prefer that he should speak first.

Guiteau—I want to be heard on that question, Your Honor. I want to close the argument for the defence. I wouldn't trust my case in the hands of the best lawyer in America."

Judge Cox—I should be loth in a capital case to deny any man a proper opportunity to be heard, even if he is represented by counsel, but in this case it is safe to assume that the prisoner will abuse the privilege, as he has done all through the trial, and that what he would say would be highly improper to go before the jury. I shall therefore deny him the privilege. As I said yesterday, however, if his counsel desire to read from his manuscript anything which they deem proper to be read before the jury they can do so.

Guiteau protested that he appeared as his own counsel, and claimed the right as an American citizen to be heard in his own defence. Finding that Judge Cox could not be moved, he shouted, "Let the record show that I appear here as my own counsel, and that I take exception to your ruling, Judge Cox. I shall appeal to the American people and they will overrule you, and you will go down to future ages with a black stain upon your name."

Judge Cox made no reply to this tirade, but simply nodded to Mr. Reed to begin his argument.

Mr. Reed then rose to address the jury on behalf of the prisoner. He commenced by paying a compliment to the jury for the seriousness, solemnity, and care which had characterized it during this long trial—a trial unparalleled in the history of criminal jurisprudence. He should not endeavor to make any statement of the evidence or to draw a gilded picture of any scene, but he would simply talk with them as between neighbors. Mr. Davidge, counsel for the prosecution, had occupied two days in addressing the jury, and that effort and consumption of time on his part showed the grave appreciation felt by the prosecution lest something might have appeared in the case which would make the jury say that this poor man was a lunatic and irresponsible.

The prisoner certainly sustained his record for impartiality in abusing and contradicting every one who had anything to say upon the case, from Judge Cox on the bench to the humblest witness on the stand. Before Colonel Reed had been speaking a half hour, the prisoner began to comment and contradict.

Contrasting the mercy of the Saviour towards those afflicted with devils (insane) with the demands of the prosecution in this case, Colonel Reed said: They say, hang him.

Guiteau shouted, "And the American people say, Let him go. The American people are on my side, Mr. Reed. Now go on with your speech."

Soon after the speaker had occasion to allude to the evidence of J. W. Guiteau, when the prisoner again interrupted and called out (disparagingly): "Well, he aint my reference. I've got better men than he is for my reference."

Col. Reed commented upon the incident related by several witnesses, when Guiteau struck his father at the supper table, and Guiteau called out vehemently: "That wasn't true. I never struck him; never intended to strike him. I don't fight any one. I am a peaceable man. If I don't like any one I tell them so and tell them to get out of the way, and that settles them."

"This act," continued the speaker, "was the first indication of his insanity. He denies it—probably he don't remember it."

Guiteau (sneeringly)—That is owing to my poor, weak mind and disordered intellect.

Colonel Reed continued—Mr. Davidge condescended to read yesterday a portion of the evidence in relation to this incident to show, as he claimed, the depravity of the prisoner, and Judge Porter kindly suggested to him that Guiteau struck his father in the back, the full record says, or neck or shoulder.

Mr. Davidge (laughingly)—Don't go back on the witness.

Colonel Reed—I am reading from the record, sir. It says——

Guiteau (with an air of satisfaction at his superior discernment)—Why, that was intended for a pun, Reed, but you don't seem to see it. I don't know as that should be wondered at, for it would require a microscope for an ordinary mortal to see it.

After the recess Mr. Reed continued his argument, reading two letters written by Guiteau at the time he left the Oneida Community, and contended that no man could read those letters and not reach the conviction that the writer was of unsound mind. This evidence was not manufactured for the occasion, it was on record years ago. Many of the experts for the Government, who had watched this prisoner closely for weeks, swore here that they did not think the prisoner, by his looks, by his talk, or by his actions here in this court room has endeavored to feign insanity.

"This," said Col. Reed, "is a point vital to this case, and I ask you, gentlemen, if a half dozen of these experts swear that he is playing a part here, and as many more swear to the contrary, and all of them witnesses for the Government, if I say these experts disagree so positively upon this point, how much weight can you attach to their opinions upon his sanity? It does not require an expert to pronounce him insane. You have seen him day after day shuffling in before you; you have seen that strange, unnatural look of his eyes, and it requires the opinion of no expert to convince you that this is not the appearance of a sane man."

Continuing in this strain the speaker said, "In my opinion if this poor creature is sent to an insane asylum, he will be a drivelling idiot within six months."

Guiteau had been quietly listening with his elbows upon the rail of the dock and his chin upon his hands, his back being turned to the audience, and his attention apparently fixed upon something in the street. This startling prediction amused him intensely. Turning round he looked over in the direction of the speaker, and enjoyed a quiet laugh for some seconds.

"These experts," said the speaker, "do not swear to a fact, for none but the inscrutable Deity can show what there is in the brain of man. They swear only to an opinion, and you have a notable instance how far from the facts the opinions of the most learned doctors may lead in the sad case of the late President. We had bulletins every day giving his condition. We had the announcement that the probe, or whatever it may be, had been inserted twelve inches into the wound, and yet the wound really led in exactly an opposite direction. I say it would be a shame to send a man to the gallows upon the opinion of doctors."

Alluding to the strictures of counsel upon the course of certain members of Guiteau's family, in sticking to the prisoner when they should have cast him off as a wretch, Mr. Reed said: "It is in evidence that, six years ago, Mrs. Scoville believed her brother a mental wreck, an insane man; and should she desert him now, that he is on trial for his life, she would be unworthy the name of sister."

During his argument Mr. Davidge had stated that, though he did not approve the mob, yet, in his opinion, "the best opinions and the highest of human motives were behind the mob."

To this sentiment Mr. Reed offered the story of the crucifixion. "Pilate was the Judge. He had said, 'I find no wrong in this man. I wash my hands of His blood;' but the mob said, 'Crucify, crucify Him.'" Referring to the difficulty experienced by the defence in securing witnesses, Col. Reed said: You can never know, gentlemen, how hard it has been to get people to come here and tell what they know. They would rather listen to the cry, "Crucify him," than come here and tell what they know to save this poor man from the gallows and the Government from the disgrace of executing an insane man.

Guiteau interrupted in loud tones, "The Government don't want me to be convicted. General Arthur don't want me to be convicted, and I aint going to be, probably." The evidence of Mr. Brooks (the chief of the Treasury detectives), who visited the prisoner in the night, and whose evidence the prosecution tried so hard to suppress, as they did the notes of Bailey, the evidence of the detective McElfresh, and in short all the evidence that might in any way aid the prisoner, Mr. Reed claimed came like a Godsend.

The morning of Monday, January 16th, witnessed the opening of the tenth week of the Guiteau trial and the beginning of Mr. Scoville's argument for the defence. The court room was densely crowded. The great trial might have begun but yesterday so far as public interest was concerned. Mr. Scoville's prophecy at the beginning of the trial that it would last ten or twelve weeks was recalled by a member of the bar and his judgment and foresight commended. It was now evident that Mr. Scoville understood his own plan from the start, and that was the dragging out of the trial in the expert evidence and cross-examination as long as possible, with the hope of entangling the jury and public in doubt and wearying the former with the whole matter. When Mr. Reed closed he said he felt satisfied, from his judgment and long experience with juries, that had the case been given to the jury at that time the verdict would have been acquittal on the ground of insanity.

During Mr. Scoville's argument John W. Guiteau was writing a letter to his wife. He allowed a correspondent to see it. In it he says: "For the last few days or week I have had a good deal of hope that the jury will disagree, if they do not actually acquit. The Judge's instructions, as he intimated when the prayers were dismissed, were made more favorable than we feared they might be, and the public sentiment has decidedly changed in favor of the fact that the prisoner is insane now and when he shot the President, July 2, 1881, and had been many years prior thereto. Hundreds and thousands of people who have attended the trial have gone away not doubting the apparent fact of insanity."

MR. SCOVILLE'S ADDRESS.

An Attack upon the Counsel for the Prosecution.

The familiar "Come to order, gentlemen; hats off," of the antique court crier announced to the eagerly expectant throng, at 10.10 in the morning, that the tenth week of the Guiteau trial was about to be entered upon. The prisoner came in smiling, with more confidence in his walk and manner than he had previously evinced. He saluted pleasantly his counsel and his brother as he passed them, and, seating himself in the dock, gave his attention at once to the morning papers, carefully scanning each to see how much space it had devoted to his speech (which we give elsewhere in this book).

Mr. Scoville arose and began his address to the jury. He appealed to the jurors to divest their minds wholly of any preconceived opinions on the case. They ought not to come to any conclusion until the last word had dropped from the Judge in his final charge. He would not attempt to appeal to the sentiments of the jury. The gentleman who would follow him (Mr. Porter) would attempt to influence their emotions; he would address himself to their hearts rather than to their intellects, and, if the question was to be decided by emotion, by passion, by prejudice, by fear, then the defendant would be hanged. But the jury under their oaths could not be influenced by any such considerations. What was the issue? It was whether or not the prisoner was insane on the 2d of July last when he shot the President.

He said that Davidge was fair and honest, but stated that, insensibly, he had not in all cases given the jury a fair, full, strict, honest statement of the evidence. Neither had he given them a full, fair, honest statement of the law. He (Scoville) would, before he concluded, take the liberty of criticising the conduct of the other counsel for the prosecution more at length, simply because they deserved it.

Charging a Conspiracy.

Mr. Scoville charged that in this case there had been a conspiracy on the part of the District Attorney, Mr. Porter, Mr. Davidge, and the expert witnesses, Drs. Hamilton, McDonald, Kempster, Gray and Worcester; and the object of the conspiracy was to hang the defendant. One of his specifications in the charge against the conspirators in the present case was that they had attempted to pervert the law. Referring to Mr. Porter's repudiation of the idea that Judge Noah Davis, of New York, sat on the same bench as Barnard and Cardoza, Mr. Scoville declared that the two latter Judges had never done a more reprehensible thing than Judge Davis did when he attempted to promulgate a judicial decision not bearing on the case before him, but intended to influence this case, with which he had nothing to do. Mr. Scoville proceeded to criticise some of Mr. Davidge's propositions in his argument to the jury, complaining of misrepresentations of the law. One of these propositions was that the case must turn on "the iron rule whether the man knew the difference between right and wrong." Mr. Scoville proceeded to argue that from the prisoner's standpoint, from his diseased view of it, the act was not wrong—it was right, and so Mr. Davidge's proposition was not a correct proposition of law. The inmate of an insane asylum when he attacked another inmate or an officer of the institution knew that he was committing a crime and knew the difference between the right and the wrong of the act, but no one ever heard of these insane people being held to account in a court of justice under this "iron rule of law." If he (Scoville) had never studied law he would still have known enough

The Act of a Diseased Mind.

Mr. Scoville cited several similar quotations from Mr. Davidge's argument in order to show that the counsel representing the prosecution were wilfully falsifying the law. It occurred some thirty times, he said, in Mr. Davidge's argument. The prisoner might have had on the 2d of July last enough sense and judgment to know that it would be wrong to pick up a pocket-book which he found on a bench in the railroad station and transfer it to his pocket. That was not the question. If the prisoner was on that morning overpowered by the consciousness (coming through his diseased mind) that the Lord was requiring him to do an act for the good of the country and to save the nation from war, then it was the result of a diseased mind and the act was, in the prisoner's view of it, right.

In the course of a further criticism of what he called Mr. Davidge's unfair presentation of the law and the testimony he was interrupted by the prisoner, who shouted: "You cannot blame Davidge for what he said; he was paid for it." On another occasion, when Mr. Scoville said that if the prosecution had anything of consequence to show against the prisoner he would not object to it, the prisoner said: "They have not got anything. They could not prove anything against me, because I am a square man."

Guiteau's Many Interruptions.

After the recess Mr. Scoville proceeded with his argument, pointing out several places in Mr. Davidge's address in which there was a deviation from or misrepresentation of the testimony. After speaking some half an hour he was interrupted by the prisoner, who said: "Davidge had better read my speech. It is published this morning—over a page of it. I must have an understanding with his Honor as to whether I shall have a chance to deliver it or not."

When Mr. Scoville praised the prosecution for bringing witnesses, at great expense, to testify to some trivial incident, the prisoner exclaimed: "That is sarcasm." Mr. Scoville proceeded with his criticism of Mr. Davidge's argument. While he was talking Attorney General Brewster entered the court room and took a seat beside Judge Cox. A good deal of time was spent over the testimony of Stephen English, the prisoner continuing to interject his own remarks. The longest of them was: "The reason I had so much trouble in getting English out of Ludlow Street Jail was that Mr. Winston and the life insurance companies knew him to be a first-class fraud, and were 'dead set' against him. He would not have got out if I had not stuck to him like a dog to a piece of meat. When I take hold of a thing I pull solid. English never got a judgment against me and never will. If I had a million dollars in my pocket I would not give the fellow a cent. That is enough on English." Subsequently, in alluding to the testimony about the non-payment of board-bills, the prisoner again interrupted him, saying: "That reminds me to say here that if these people to whom I owe little bills will send them in they can get their money now. I have got the means to pay them. I owe about a thousand dollars, and that, I suppose, is not to hang a man." Referring to Shaw's testimony as to the incident of the oroide watch, Scoville said (ironically): "And this is another step in the vast career of crime which leads on to the gallows." "That is good," said the prisoner; "but you had better dismiss Shaw with a 'pshaw' and let him go."

As no laugh followed he spelled out the word, and said: "They do not see the pun, do they?" Referring to the testimony of Shaw and of his clerk, as to the conversation in which the prisoner said he would imitate Wilkes Booth, Mr. Scoville declared his belief that in that matter both those witnesses had perjured themselves. ["I know that they have," said the prisoner.] Shaw wanted to bring this man to the gallows. He (Scoville) could honor Mason, McGill and Jones, as compared with Shaw. They were willing to take their lives in their hands, if necessary. They were willing, at least, to stake their personal liberty on the issue. But Shaw sought to hang this man without assuming even the risk of a prosecution for perjury.

"This whole Shaw business," the prisoner interrupted, "is a lie from beginning to end, and any decent man will say so."

Then (as the Court was declared adjourned at three o'clock) Guiteau said: "I ask your Honor to read my speech this evening, because I want to talk to you about it to-morrow morning."

In spite of the very unpropitious weather on the morning of the 17th the court room contained its usual crowd of spectators, the ladies being largely in the majority. The prisoner sat quietly in the dock for some minutes, but when Mr. Scoville rose to proceed with his argument the prisoner reminded him that he was to address the Court, and Mr. Scoville yielded for that purpose. The prisoner then proceeded to read, in a very pretentious, oratorical style, a plea to the Court to allow him to read his speech to the jury. "In general," he said, "I am satisfied with the law as proposed by your Honor, but I have suggested a still broader view, which I ask your Honor to follow, to wit: That if the jury believe that I believed it was right to remove the President, because I had special Divine authority so to do, and was forced to do it by the Deity, they will acquit on the ground of transitory mania." He went on to say that neither Mr. Reed nor Mr. Scoville had represented him. He knew his own feelings and his inspiration, "And I ask your Honor," he continued, "in the name of justice, in the name of the American people, to allow me to address the jury of my countrymen, when my life may be at stake. If a man on that jury has a doubt as to his duty in acquitting me, my speech will probably settle him in my favor."

Mr. Scoville Complains.

Mr. Scoville then proceeded with his argument, criticising the District Attorney for sending experts to the jail, not to find out the true state of Guiteau's mind, but to make out a case for the Government. Mr. Scoville complained that the District Attorney had suppressed all evidence of the state of the prisoner's mind for the first two weeks since his confinement. He complained also that Mr. Davidge had misrepresented the testimony of Dr. Spitzka, and that all the counsel for the Government had sought by ridicule to belittle Dr. Spitzka and to do away with the effect of his open, manly, scientific statements. That was conduct worthy of a police court rather than of this court. Referring to the refusal of the prosecution to allow the defence to examine Detective McElfresh and Dr. McFarland and Clark Mills, Mr. Scoville said he did not want to hear any more of a fair and impartial trial. He criticised the course of the prosecution in refusing to permit the prisoner to address the jury for a brief hour or two, simply because they fear he might disclose by his manner or speech his true mental condition. Referring to Mr. Porter, he spoke of him as having come here for money, and lent himself to the practices which he (Mr. Scoville) had been describing. He alluded to his rising up with all the dignity of Demosthenes to discuss some small questions of evidence, and he confessed to have resorted to some little subterfuges to draw Mr. Porter out. He had done so to such purpose that Mr. Porter had trained his big guns on himself (Scoville), and to-day Mr. Porter would make as strong a speech against him and would condemn him as strongly as Guiteau.

The Prisoner—He would be in favor of hanging you.

An Attack on Porter.

Mr. Scoville—Mr. Porter, carried away by the heat of his passion, denounced the whole tribe of Guiteaus who sympathized with the defendant, and he just stopped in his expression when he wanted to consign us all to the gallows. That is the kind of man that Mr. Porter is; and when he comes before you with his tremendous efforts, with his long, bony finger pointing now at this juryman and now at another, commanding them to find this man guilty and urging it with all the force which he can command as the last expiring effort of a long life of forensic eloquence which shall hand his name down to the ages as an advocate, remember, gentlemen, that back of all this is a large fee; back of it all is Mr. Porter's personal feeling,

Guiteau under the shadow of the gallows. "Comment unnecessary."
Guiteau dem Galgen nahe.—Bedarf feiner Erklärung.

not against the prisoner only, but against me and the Guiteau family; and back of all this is the fact Mr. Porter has come here to prostitute his talents and his high attainments for money to hang an insane man. As to the District Attorney, he has been dictatorial throughout this case. He has treated the defendant's witnesses with all the domineering, overbearing conduct of a Jeffreys. He has attempted to carry this case for the prosecution by conduct unbecoming his high office. And if this man be hanged, if he goes to the gallows, through the efforts of the District Attorney of this District, through his suppression of evidence, through the arts and devices which have characterized this prosecution and which have been a disgrace to it, then, in after years, if conscience does its duty, that scene will come very often before the imagination of the gentleman. And in the night time the vision will come to him of a black form hanging by the neck. The voice will come to him from beneath the black cap drawn over that shapeless head and it will say, in the tones of a lunatic: "It was God's act, Corkhill, not mine," and he will not be able to escape it. He may now seek to ride on the wave of popular revenge a conquering hero, but it will be like the case of the Parisian mob which crowned a harlot and called her their goddess. And when the reaction comes and the wave subsides he will be left stranded on the barren shore of popular opinion, an object of disgrace.

"Thank you, sir," said the District Attorney, smiling sarcastically.

Mr. Scoville then went on to give the theory of the defence. He thought that the prisoner was affected with chronic insanity and that the commencement of it was when the prisoner was a boy of about nineteen years of age or before that.

A Fortune for Guiteau.

After the recess the prisoner opened the proceedings by saying, "I am in good luck this morning. I have just received a check for $25,000 on the First National Bank of New York; another check for $5,000, and still another for $750. I believe them all to be good checks, too. I wish to send my thanks to the givers, and I hope this thing will be kept up."

Mr. Scoville then resumed his address to the jury. He attributed to transitory mania the incident of the prisoner's raising an axe against his sister and the circumstance of his denying it, because such sudden attacks of transitory mania were frequently accompanied by total forgetfulness. He reviewed the prisoner's life down to the time when he entered the Oneida Community. His whole conduct in the Community was the outgrowth of an intense, uncontrollable religious element.

Mr. Scoville was sure that when the jury came to weigh all the considerations, when they came to understand truly and correctly the mental condition of this man, they would not consider it unusual or out of place that the political situation (to which the prisoner had referred them so often) was the moving cause of unhinging his intellect and dethroning his reason. He had got the idea from a man high in party council—Senator Chandler, of Michigan—that another civil war would come in which millions of men would be sacrificed, and the thought came to him: "Can that calamity be averted?" That thought was supplemented by another. "Yes, it can be averted by the removal of the President. If the President were out of the way these troubles would cease." His next idea was, "Perhaps I am the divinely-appointed agent to accomplish it." Then entirely consistent with his whole life he immediately goes to the Lord in prayer to find out whether the suggestion was a good or an evil one, whether it came from God or the devil. Of course any sane man would have known that the Lord would not prompt him to kill another man, but no one could judge as to the workings of an insane mind. After two weeks' prayer he had become convinced that the Lord required him to do this act and then he went on day by day deliberating to do what he believed the Lord required him to do. From his standpoint he knew that from the very nature of things the act could not be wrong.

Guiteau's Own Defence.

If the prisoner, Mr. Scoville continued

had been allowed to address the jury he would have taken the position that his act in shooting the President was right; that it was commanded by God; that it was such an act as only infinite wisdom could have divined and infinite power accomplished in order to save this country, and that he was the humble instrument in the hands of God in doing it. That would have been his plea if he could have made his speech. What do you think of that, gentlemen of the jury, as the indication of a sound mind? It would be simply saying to you: "The Lord did this thing; if you are going to hang anybody hang the Deity, the principal actor; I was only the instrument in his hand." How different that is, gentlemen, from the real defence in this case. We say that the prisoner never had any inspiration of any kind; that the Lord never required him to remove the dead President; that it was a falsehood and delusion from the beginning, and that it was in its inception and execution and is to-day a proof of the diseased mind of this man.

The Prisoner—You and the American people do not agree on that, my friend. They are coming to my side and do not you forget it.

The Court here at 3.45 P. M., adjourned.

Mr. Scoville's Sensation.

On Wednesday morning, January 18th, Mr. Scoville got off a tirade that is believed to have injured his case with the jury.

It was a severe, and by many said to have been an entirely uncalled for attack on the "Stalwarts," including such prominent persons as President Arthur, General Grant and ex-Senator Roscoe Conkling. His speech on this day was very bitter indeed.

Every seat in the court room was occupied and all available standing room. The Court having been called to order the prisoner said in a quiet tone, different in every respect from the one which he used when he made his usual morning speech: "I hope Your Honor will allow me to address the jury after Mr. Scoville gets through." "I will consider that after Mr. Scoville has finished," replied Judge Cox. Mr. Scoville then proceeded with his address.

He commented upon the testimony of Dr. Gray, of the Utica Asylum, and cited cases of insanity stated in tables made out by him to show that persons committed homicides under insane delusions and soon afterwards sustained a reaction and could converse in an intelligent manner. These tables show that in cases of homicidal mania the patient was not always past recovery. The prisoner had honestly acted under a delusion, which delusion was his belief that the Lord required him to do the act; but that, as soon as the reaction came, he feeling that he had done what the Lord required had gone to the jail as a place of rest or repose. In that repose he had remained up to the time of the trial. He contended that the prisoner had not been playing a part, but had pursued the very opposite course. He had said and done much to prejudice the theory of insanity. If he had been sane and playing insanity he would not have done this. "When anything strikes him as wrong," said Mr. Scoville, "he says so at once, and here is the secret of his just denunciations of the District Attorney, the man who introduced spies into his cell to obtain his secrets and, if possible, to hang him. But, thank God, they never obtained one item of evidence which would operate against him. You yourselves, gentlemen of the jury, have seen how this honorable District Attorney has wickedly suppressed and destroyed evidence that would have aided the prisoner."

Guiteau. That last is meant for sarcasm.

The Infamy of the Politicians.

At this point of his address Mr. Scoville branched off to the question of politics as connected with the case and his remarks were listened to with great deal of attention and interest. He said: If there were no reasons back of this prosecution, this man arraigned here before you, gentlemen, would never have been brought into a court of justice. He would have been taken, after the homicide, to an insane asylum, and kept there until he died Back of this prosecution is something which I have had to contend against and which you may now or will feel the pressure of before you get through with the case. It is not merely the efforts of this man (pointing to the District Attorney). Back of him is the United States government; and I arraign before you, gentlemen, as those who are crowding the prisoner to the gallows persons high in authority. I say, and I say it without fear, that the movers of this prosecution are those politicians who seek to hide their own infamy by casting the blame on this insane man. I say that such men as Conkling and Grant and Arthur—those who made war without justification on that dead President, whom they have since lauded to the skies—instituted that state of things and manufactured that degree of public excitement and political feeling that preyed on this insane man until reason left its throne and did that which he considered to be perfectly in accordance with their counsel and their conduct. I did not intend to say this when I opened the case. Then I expected a fair and impartial trial. I supposed that there would be no effort on the part of the prosecution, on the part of the gentleman who represents the United States Government, to prevent it from introducing all proper evidence. I supposed that I would have the poor pittance which I asked for and which, as an American citizen, I was entitled to, which every criminal is entitled to until the jury brings in the verdict. I supposed that we would have that which I came to Washington for, to wit, a fair and impartial trial of this case.

Assaulting the Stalwarts.

But since I have found that the evidence has been suppressed, that every undue advantage has been taken that could be taken by the prosecution, I have come to the conclusion that I shall not spare these men who fomented this strife and permit them to make a scapegoat of this insane man so that they shall still be revered and honored in public estimation. What I have to say is this, and I say it without any feeling or if there is any feeling it is one of regret, that men placed so high in power, elevated so high by the suffrages of their fellow-citizens as those persons are, should forget their high duties and descend from the high positions in which they have been placed to the petty and ignominious scramble for office which was exhibited in the warfare waged on President Garfield. Do you believe that this crime would ever have been committed if Conkling and Platt had not resented the nomination by President Garfield of Judge Robertson to be Collector of the port of New York? He sees a President whom, since his death, all say to be one of the noblest of the land. I say it because I believe it and because I had that opinion of him before his death. But these men who, since his death, have been so profuse in their admiration of him, who have said so many things in laudation of his character and his high motives, were ready before the second of July last to trample him in the dust if they had had the opportunity. They were ready to degrade and disgrace him with his country. They were ready to see him go down to obscurity and disgrace to the grave, if it could be done without the aid of an assassin's hand.

Conkling shall not Escape.

I admit that Mr. Conkling is (imitating Mr. Porter's style of declamation) "one of the first parliamentarians of the age," that he is a great statesman. I admit that, and Mr. Conkling, with those qualities had no right, had no business to engage in a petty squabble about a petty office. He waged a war on the chosen representative of the American people in the Presidential chair. Mr. Conkling shall not shirk, shall not avoid, shall not escape the condemnation of the American people, if I can fasten it on him, for that disgraceful conduct on his part. Neither shall General Grant, honored as he is by his country, honored as he has been by the suffrages of the people, honored as he has been for twenty years in my own heart—neither shall General Grant escape that condemnation to which he justly subjected himself when, coming from Mexico, leaving his duties and coming with undue haste, he threw his own name and influence into that petty quarrel about a small office in the Republican party, and sought to foment the difference which had sprung up. General Grant stands only a nobleman as he stands in the hearts of his countrymen. We have no Lord Grant, no

Duke of Galena; we have only General Grant, and as long as he maintains the high character, his devotion to his country, so long and no longer will he maintain that place which he has obtained in the hearts of his countrymen. It is more noble for General Grant to say what he has lately said in relation to General Porter, that his conduct toward him eighteen years ago was a mistake, that he did a wrong and that it should be corrected—it was more noble, more manly in him to take that position than to do anything which he has accomplished during the course of his long life.

Arthur's Condemnation.

But there is another step for him to take and another step for the President to take if they would redeem themselves in the opinion of their countrymen. When the Vice-President of the United States left his high position and went to Albany and prostituted his place and his talent and his influence towards the fomenting and spreading of this quarrel and controversy in the Republican party he deserved the condemnation of every citizen of this Republic. And that conduct sticks to him yet and will until he and General Grant and Senator Conkling, in all their pride, in all their ambition, shall come out openly and plainly before the public, through a letter or declaration of some kind, and say that this warfare which they waged on President Garfield was unwarranted and was disgraceful to them as citizens of the Republic, holding the high positions which they held. I say this thing on my own responsibility. I would not have said it now, but further—I am not going to see the shortcomings and the misdeeds of these men, though high in place and power, visited on the head of this insane man if I can help it. And I tell you how it would be done—if you find a verdict of guilty. This is the reason which had prompted all this expenditure of power and force on the part of the administration to hang this man. This is it. It is not for the purpose of vindicating President Garfield. It is not for the purpose of doing justice. But if it can be made to appear by the verdict of a jury that this act was the act of a sane man, a man who was responsible for his conduct, by a man who could conceal his action, a man who should be judged by the same standard by which we judge ourselves, what then? Why, these men can say, and will say, "We are not responsible for what a sane man has done. We are not responsible for that. It is true we had a quarrel; it is true we had a difference, but no sane man had a right because of that to shoot the President." And that reasoning is perfectly correct. Therefore, if you find this prisoner guilty these men are sheltered, screened, almost vindicated from public opinion. But, on the other hand, suppose you find this man not guilty by reason of insanity, what is the result? The people say: "This is the man whose mind was preyed upon by supposed impending evil; who was led to believe that there was another war coming, and that a million lives were to be sacrificed. Under that delusion he shot the President of the United States." That will be the first conclusion. What will be the next step? Somebody must be to blame when an act of this kind has been done. Who induced this poor lunatic to do this act? Recollect those slips cut from the newspapers and stating what Conkling said, what Conkling did, what Arthur said, what Arthur did, what Grant said, what Grant did. When the people make up their minds they will fix the blame somewhere. Where will it rest but upon the heads of and hearts of those men who waged this unjustifiable war against the dead President? And these men will rest forever with that opprobrium upon them, and they will go down to their graves with the contempt and reproach of their fellow-citizens, unless they do the only thing that can be done —what Grant has done in relation to Fitz John Porter—come out and say as American citizens: "We did wrong." Let them write a letter to the desolate widow at Cleveland and say to her: "It is true we are sorry; it is true we mourn with you; but we feel that this terrible calamity was in some degree the outgrowth, the legitimate result of this unjustifiable war which we waged against your dead husband, and we pray you to forgive us." When these men do that they will show their claim to the regard of the American people, and it is the only thing they can do to save their names from merited oblivion.

Some Remarks from Guiteau.

After the recess the prisoner opened the proceedings with a desire to talk a little about politics, too. "There are," he asserted, "two or three crank newspapers in the country, to wit: Reid's *Tribune*, Medill's Chicago *Tribune*, Halstead's Cincinnati *Commercial*, George William Curtis, the man milliner. The weather has been rather cool lately. These fellows had better be off under the trees and cool off a little. The only cranks in the country are those fellows. They had better join the Grant-Guiteau-Arthur combination, and get into good company and become good Republicans."

There were several exciting scenes. The court room was packed as usual, the male sex, outside of counsel and reporters, being represented by not more than a score. All the rest of the audience was composed of ladies. One lady, weighing close to three hundred pounds, pressed in, and finding a vacant spot with three or four unoccupied chairs about her quickly and quietly sat down, doubtless wondering why the chairs remained untaken. She soon found out when an officer informed her that she was in the dock. With a quick remark she arose to leave, and the officer attempted to assist her over the rail into a chair beyond. The lady got one foot and limb over, but could not draw the other after her. Two policemen and a deputy marshal went to her assistance, and amid great laughter she was finally elevated sufficiently to pass the rail and to settle in the chair beyond. Officer Cunningham, who assisted in the lifting, declared that she weighed four hundred if she weighed a pound.

Assaulting a Guard.

When the Court took a recess another exciting scene occurred. The prisoner was very impatient to get out of the dock, and scarcely could keep still long enough to be handcuffed. Captain Tall did not wish to take him into the crowd, and Guiteau showed ugliness and temper because he was not permitted to go right out. The delay did not exceed two minutes, and then the officers started with him. When he reached the counsel table he stopped and exchanged a few words with his brother. The guards then moved on with him, and when he got around where the jury sits he made another halt to talk again with some gentlemen. The crowd was pressing around and behind him, and Captain Tall, wishing to escape it, pushed his prisoner along. This made him mad and he turned quickly and shot out both hands, planting his fists in the deputy marshal's breast. The officers quickly turned on him and hustled him out in double quick time and up stairs to the private room, where he was wrathy for a few minutes and pronounced the deputy marshal an unmitigated nuisance. Captain Tall gave him very quickly to understand that he was in his charge and if he would not conduct himself decently he would be compelled to do so. If he wanted force resorted to he would get it to his heart's content. Hardly had the prisoner got up stairs before Mrs. Scoville was on the spot and sided with the prisoner. The scene in the court room took place near the door and was done so quickly that only the persons in the immediate vicinity saw it.

Mr. Scoville finished his speech at two o'clock and was applauded for his effort. It was acknowledged that for his inexperience in criminal law he conducted his case with ability. He was harassed at almost every turn by the sneers of the District Attorney. It was agreed on this day that Guiteau should be allowed to address the jury.

Judge Porter for the Prosecution.

It might be well to state just here that Judge Porter is an *ex-Judge*, and employed as a lawyer by the prosecution. It is apt to prove confusing to those of our readers not familiar with these facts. In other words, it is well to bear in mind that there was really but *one* Judge in this case—Judge Cox, who presided.

For every seat in the court room on the morning of the 23d there were at least ten clamoring applicants besieging every avenue of approach. Members of the press, counsel and court officers found the greatest difficulty in forcing their way through the throngs that blocked up every passage-way. Even the holders of special tickets were in many instances unable to get near enough to the policemen and bailiffs to show them their credentials. At half-past nine the doors were opened, and in an incredibly short space of time every nook in the room was filled, and the doors were again closed. Several hundred, perhaps a thousand, people were shivering upon the outside, and many of them still remained at the hour of recess. After the usual warning by Marshal Henry, the court was duly opened, and the prisoner brought in.

As soon as seated Guiteau opened the day's proceedings with the following announcement: "I spent yesterday in examining my mail. I had several hundred letters, many of them from ladies, and some were very tender. I desire to express my thanks to the ladies for these kind and tender letters. One letter suggests that General Arthur give me a Cabinet office. Now, I want to say, I would not take any office from President Arthur, and, under the circumstances, I don't think it proper that I should accept one.

"Now, in regard to Judge Porter, I want to say: As he is to have the closing of the case, if he attempts to mislead the Court or the jury, I and my counsel will stop him. He came into this case under a misapprehension on the part of General Arthur, otherwise he would not be in the case. He don't properly represent the Government. He only represents himself."

Judge Porter entered the court room shortly before the prisoner had delivered himself of this warning. After a moment's delay he stepped to the open space before the jury, and in tones which clearly betrayed his weakened condition, began the closing argument upon this now celebrated case.

Said Judge Porter: "If it please your Honor and gentlemen of the jury, in my infirmity—for I share your fatigue—I proceed as best I can to discharge my duty.

"The nature of this duty is such that I should feel that I were almost an accessory after the fact if I should fail to say such words as I can to aid you in reaching a proper conclusion. Thus far the trial has practically been conducted by the prisoner and Mr. Scoville. Every one has been denounced at their will, and even now I am informed that I will be interrupted by them both."

Judge Porter briefly recited the scenes of disorder, the abuse and slander to which every one upon the case had for two months been subjected, and yet, he said, of the three speeches which had been made by the defence, I will do the prisoner the justice to say that his was the least objectionable. After sketching the circumstances leading up to the crime, and painting with fervid language the damning wickedness of its execution, Judge Porter turned his attention to the prisoner, and proceeded to depict his character:

A beggar, a hypocrite, a robber, and a swindler, a lawyer who never won a cause—no Court, no jury failed to see in him the dishonest rogue, and such men cannot win causes—he has left his trail of infamy in a hundred directions. The man who, as a lawyer, had such notions of morality that when he had taken debts to collect and collected them by dogging the debtor, he held them against his client; a man who was capable of blasting the name of the woman with whom he had slept for years, and still recognized as his wife; a man who, when he tired of this woman, pretending to be a Christian and a believer of the Bible, looked in the book and read, "Thou shalt not commit adultery," and then went out and deliberately committed adultery with a street-walker; a man who pushed himself into the fellowship of Christian associations as a follower of the Saviour, when fresh from six years of foul fornication in the Oneida Community.

Guiteau—"That lie ought to choke you."

As Judge Porter proceeded with the resistless torrent of denunciation and invective the prisoner occasionally called out, "That's a lie," "That's absolutely false," or "That aint so."

Passing in review the principal events of the prisoner's life, Judge Porter showed up in all its hideous deformity, the infamous bent of his nature. Alluding to his dispute with his brother, John

JUDGE COX, PRESIDING.

W. Guiteau, in Boston, when he struck the latter in the face, Judge Porter said: "This was the first and the last time this coward ever struck any blow in the face. His coward hand always struck from behind."

After showing who and what was the murderer, Judge Porter next described his victim, paying a glowing tribute to the character and services of the lamented President, and pronouncing a most touching eulogy, as it were, upon his memory. The claims of the prisoner to be a praying man were considered, and the hollow mockery of the claim was shown.

Guiteau angrily shouted: "I pray every night and morning and before every meal. If you did the same you would be a better man. You wouldn't be here looking for blood money."

The prisoner says he prayed for six weeks. Why, if he had made up his mind unalterably to murder the President on the first of June, said Judge Porter, did he still continue to pray down to the very act of murder?

Guiteau—"I prayed to see if the Lord wouldn't let me off from killing him."

What was he praying for? continued Judge Porter. The man who claimed to have received a Divine inspiration himself prepares his defence in advance for an act to which he was Divinely inspired. The believer in inspiration, he would himself alter the inspired book and substitute for it a book of his own. That he did not shoot the President on the first occasion, said Judge Porter, was due to his coward heart. Had he done it on that occasion he would have been torn to pieces, and he knew it. On this occasion the President was surrounded by his Cabinet and his friends. His son —not yet strong, but who would have been urged at such a time with God-given strength to defend his father— was also by his side, and the assassin's craven heart failed him and he said, "Not yet; at some other time."

With graphic picturing, Judge Porter related the dogging of the President's footsteps to the little church, the incidents or accidents which on each occasion baffled him. President Garfield's visit to Secretary Blaine's house, dogged by the assassin, was vividly portrayed.

It was night, said the speaker, dark as that night when the devil first whispered this crime in the assassin's ear. He lay hiding in the alley. Why? With the inspired command of God resting upon him to kill the President, and with a pressure that would have made him do it if he died the next minute, at any time after June 1st. Why did he not kill him then? Because he says it was too hot, and he thought he would do it some other time. Because this politician thought he could become the idol of the Stalwarts and of the Republican party. Because he thought he had so carefully laid the foundation for his defence against the crime, and for his protection from mob violence, that he might safely commit the act in the light of day. This careful man—careful of his own safety—made every provision, even to his conveyance to the jail, and after he had seen his victim fall turned and ran—ran where? Where could he run?

Mr. Scoville, interrupting Judge Porter, said: "I desire to correct the speaker on the evidence. I do not find a single witness who testified that the prisoner ran after the firing."

Mr. Davidge, with earnestness, objected to the interruption. He believed it but the first of a series of interruptions intended to break the force of the closing argument. Counsel has no right to interrupt unless the speaker read incorrectly.

Judge Cox—We cannot have a running discussion, and that is just what this will lead to.

Mr. Scoville—I was interrupted 147 times. I have done so but twice. I propose to test this question right here, if counsel persists in misrepresentations.

Mr. Davidge—Your Honor can at once see the object of this thing, and it is for your Honor to decide whether the argument is to be given in its entirety to the jury, or whether it is to be split up in this manner.

Judge Cox—You will proceed, Judge Porter.

The speaker, after this somewhat breezy incident, continued by saying: I cannot in this argument even allude to Mr. Scoville or Mr. Reed, the counsel upon the other side. This case looms up so immeasurably above them that, in making the closing argument, I cannot even allude to them, except as it may be absolutely necessary.

The evidence and the papers presented here by General Reynolds, said Judge Porter, and among them the prisoner's address to the American people, are sufficient to stamp him a cool, calculating, cold-blooded murderer. These papers at one time could not be found, either in the District Attorney's or Attorney General's offices, and neither of the counsel for the Government saw them until a day or two before General Reynolds took the stand. But, thank God, the papers were found, and they are in evidence before you, and, before I conclude, I think I shall be able to show you that not one of you could, upon this evidence, acquit this criminal, unless you perjure your souls, and assume your share of responsibility for the murder of the lamented Garfield.

Guiteau—That's all bosh. I'm very glad those papers are here. When the Attorney General saw them he would not have anything to do with the case.

Judge Porter then explained at some length the relations of counsel for the prosecution to this case, in reply, as he said, to the frequent insinuations of the prisoner and his counsel that he (Porter) and his associates were improperly influenced by the expectation of money reward and had entered into a conspiracy to execute the law and convict this prisoner. The District Attorney's duty was plain and his salary fixed by law, and, said Judge Porter, it is simply $2,000 a year and fees in certain cases as prescribed by law.

Guiteau shouted: "His office, I'm told, is worth $7,000 a year, and yet he can't pay his board bills. He spends it all for wine and fancy women."

Speaking of his own compensation, Judge Porter said that was a matter to be fixed and determined by the highest law officer of the Government, and whether the prisoner was convicted or acquitted would make no difference if his full duty in this responsible charge was performed. In reply to the broadcast imputation put upon the Government witnesses, that they were offered special inducements by Colonel Corkhill to come here and testify, Judge Porter said not one dollar can Colonel Corkhill draw from the Treasury except upon proper vouchers, certified according to law, and not a single witness has received one dollar more than the bare allowance provided by law.

Judge Porter repelled the assumption of the counsel for the defence that there was a man upon the jury who would hang the jury. The prisoner himself had indicated that he rested his safety upon one man——

Guiteau—I rely on twelve men.

The arguments for the defence for the past seven days had all been directed to divide the jury. Judge Porter addressed himself upon this subject with great force of argument and eloquence directly to the intelligence and conscience of the jury. They must not believe, if any man of them thought to discharge his duty, by avoiding a full duty, and should cause a divided jury, that the United States Government would any the less press this case to a conviction. Judge Porter continued: This case stands and stands alone upon the single question whether, on the 2d of July, the prisoner believed he was commanded to commit this crime.

Guiteau—That's it, and that's all there is in it.

Judge Porter—The prisoner asserts, and, in my opinion, he knew from the first that upon this sole issue must his case rest. If his counsel had half the intelligence of the prisoner they would have seen the same.

Guiteau—Thank you, Judge, but I don't take much stock in your opinion any way.

Judge Porter adverted to the constant interruptions of the prisoner, his false claims of sympathy, and that the press was with him, and said in contradiction, I have yet to see a single American newspaper that has one word to say in his defence.

Mr. Scoville vainly strove to get the ear of the Court, protesting that Judge Porter was exceeding the rules of the court by such statements. At length Judge Porter paused, and Mr. Scoville demanded that he be allowed to make similar statements in reply. Judge Porter attempted to go on, but Mr. Scoville, reinforced by the clamor of the prisoner, succeeded in getting the floor, when, with much excitement, he demanded that his rights, and he claimed that he had rights, should be respected. He insisted that Judge Porter had no right to state what the newspapers said or what they did not say, and he desired an exception duly noted.

Col. Corkhill insisted that counsel had a right to object; the prisoner had been allowed to state what he had received in the way of letters; he had been permitted to read them; to read extracts from the papers, and to make all sorts of statements as to what the American people and press were saying of him. Judge Porter was simply contradicting these statements.

Judge Cox intimated that the prisoner was not allowed to do as charged, but could not be restrained from doing so.

Mr. Scoville—Well, can't Judge Porter be restrained?

Judge Cox ruled that the speaker might contradict assertions of the kind made by the prisoner.

Judge Porter read from the printed evidence several of the more noted examples of this effort on the part of the prisoner to deceive the jury, after which he desired to be excused from further speaking for the day.

The Court then, at 1.15, adjourned.

Judge Cox's Charge to the Jury.

He commenced by saying that the Constitution provides that, in all criminal prosecutions, the accused shall enjoy the right of a speedy and public trial by an impartial jury, in the State or District where the crime shall have been committed; that he shall be informed of the cause and the nature of the accusation against him; that he shall be confronted with the witnesses against him; that he shall have compulsory process to obtain witnesses in his favor; and that he shall have assistance of counsel to his defence. Those provisions were intended for the protection of the innocent from injustice and oppression; and it was only by their faithful observance that guilt or innocence could be fairly ascertained. Every accused person was presumed to be innocent until the accusation was proved. With what difficulty and trouble the law had been administered in the present case the jurors had been daily witnesses. It was, however, a consolation to think, that not one of these said guarantees of the Constitution had been violated in the person of the accused. At last the long chapter of proof was ended; the task of the advocate was done, and it now rested with the jury to determine the issue between public justice and the prisoner at the bar. No one could feel more keenly than himself the great responsibility of his duties, and he felt that he could only discharge them by close adherence to the law as laid down by its highest authorities.

Before proceeding further he wished to notice an incident which had taken place pending the recent argument. The prisoner had frequently taken occasion to proclaim that public opinion, as evidenced by the press and correspondence, was in his favor. Those declarations could not have been prevented, except by the process of gagging the prisoner. Any suggestion that the jury could be influenced by such lawless clattering of the prisoner would have seemed to him absurd, and he should have felt that he was insulting the intelligence of the jury if he had not warned them not to regard it. Counsel for the prosecution had felt it necessary, however, in the final argument to interpose a contradiction to such statements, and an exception had been taken on the part of the accused to the form in which that effort was made. For the sole purpose of purging the record of any objectionable matter he should simply say that anything which had been said on either side in reference to public excitement or to newspaper opinion was not to be regarded by the jury.

The indictment charged the defendant with having murdered James A. Garfield, and it was the duty of the Court to explain the nature of the crime charged. Murder was committed where a person of sound memory and discretion unlawfully killed a reasonable being, in the peace of the United States, with malice aforethought. It had to be proved, first, that the death was caused by the act of the accused; and, further, that it was caused with malice aforethought. That did not mean, however, that the Government had to prove any ill-will or hatred on the part of the accused toward the deceased. Wherever a homicide was shown to have been committed, without lawful authority and with deliberate intent, it was sufficiently proved to have been done with malice aforethought; and malice was not disproved by showing that the accused had no personal ill-will to the deceased, and that he killed him from other motives, as, for instance, robbery or through mistaking him for another, or (as claimed in this case) to produce a public benefit. If it could be shown that the killing occurred in a heat of passion, or under provocation, then it would appear that there was no premeditated attempt, and, therefore, no malice aforethought; and that would reduce the crime to manslaughter. It was hardly necessary, however, to say that there was nothing of that kind in the present case. The jury would have to say either that the defendant was guilty of murder or that he was innocent. In order to constitute the crime of murder the assassin must have a reasonably sane mind—in technical terms, he must be "of sound mind, memory and discretion." An irresponsible, insane man could not commit murder. If he was laboring under a disease of the mental faculties to such an extent that he did not know what he was doing, or did not know it was wrong, then he was wanting in that sound mind, memory and discretion that was a part of the definition of murder. In the next place every defendant was presumed innocent until the accusation against him was established by proof. In the next place, notwithstanding this presumption of innocence, it was equally true that a defendant was presumed to be sane, and to have been so at the time the crime was committed. That is to say, that the Government was not bound to show affirmatively, as a part of its proofs, that the defendant was sane. As insanity was the exception, and as the majority of men are sane, the law presumed the latter condition of every man, until some reason was shown to believe the contrary. The burden was, therefore, on the defendant, who set up insanity as an excuse for crime, to produce proofs in the first instance to show that that presumption was mistaken, so far as it related to the prisoner. Crime, therefore, involved three elements: the killing, malice, and a responsible mind in the murderer. After all the evidence was before the jury, if the jury, while bearing in mind both these presumptions (that is, that the defendant is innocent till he is proved guilty, and that he is sane till the contrary appears), still entertained what is called a reasonable doubt on any ground or as to any of the essential elements of the crime, then the defendant was entitled to the benefit of such a doubt. It was important to explain to the jury, in the best way that the Court could, what is a reasonable doubt. He could hardly venture to give an exact definition of the term, for he did not know of any successful attempt to do so. As to questions relating to human affairs, a knowledge of which is derived from testimony, it was impossible to have the same kind of certainty that is created by scientific demonstration. The only certainty that the jury could have was a moral certainty, depending on the confidence which the jury had in the integrity of witnesses and in their capacity and opportunity to know the truth. If, for example, facts not improbable in themselves were attested by numerous witnesses, credible and uncontradicted, and who had every opportunity to know the truth, a reasonable or moral certainty would be inspired by that testimony. In such a case doubt would be unreasonable, or imaginary, or speculative. It ought not to be a doubt as to whether the party might not be innocent in the face of strong proof of his guilt, but must be a sincere doubt whether he had been proved guilty. Even where the testimony was contradictory, and where so much more credit should be given to one side than the other, the same result might be produced. On the other hand, the opposing proofs might be so balanced that the jury might justly doubt on which side, under all the circumstances, the truth lay, and in such case, the accused party was entitled to the benefit of the doubt. All that a jury could be expected to do was to be reasonably and morally certain of the facts which they declared to be their verdict.

In illustration of this point, Judge Cox quoted the charge of Chief Justice Shaw, of Massachusetts, in the case of the Commonwealth vs. Webster. With reference to the evidence in this case, very little comment was required by the Court, except upon one question, the others being hardly matters of dispute. That the defendant fired at and shot the deceased President was abundantly proved. That the wound was fatal had been testified to by the surgeons, who were competent to speak; and they were uncontradicted. That the homicide was committed with malice aforethought (if the defendant were capable of criminal intent or malice) could hardly be gainsaid. It was not necessary to prove that any special or express hatred or malice was entertained by the accused toward the deceased. It was sufficient to prove that the act was done by deliberate intent, as distinct from an act done under a certain impulse, in the heat of blood, and without previous malice. Evidence had been exhibited to the jury tending to show that the defendant admitted in his own handwriting that he had conceived the idea of "removing the President," as he called it, six weeks before the shooting; that he had deliberated upon it, and come to a determination to do it; and that about two weeks before he accomplished it he stationed himself at certain points to do the act, but for some reason was prevented. His preparation for it by the purchase of the pistol had been shown. All these facts come up to the full measure of the proof required to establish what the law denominated malice aforethought. The jury would find little difficulty in reaching a conclusion as to all the elements that made up the crime charged in the indictment, except it might be, as to the one of sound mind, memory and discretion, but that was only a technical expression for a responsible, sane man. He now approached that difficult question. He had already said that a man who is insane, in the sense that makes him irresponsible, cannot commit a crime. The defence of insanity had been so abused as to be brought into great discredit. It was the last resort in cases of unquestioned guilt. It had been an excuse for juries to bring in a verdict for acquittal when there was a public sympathy for the accused, and especially when there was provocation for the homicide according to the public sentiment, but not according to law. For that reason the defence of insanity was viewed with disfavor and public sentiment was hostile to it. Nevertheless, if insanity were established to a degree necessary, it was a perfect defence for an indictment for murder, and must be allowed full weight. It would be observed that in this case there was no trouble with any question about what might be called total insanity, such as raving mania or absolute imbecility, in which all exercise of reason is wanting and where there is no recognition of persons or things or their relations. But there was a debatable border line between sanity and insanity, and there was often great difficulty in determining on which side of this line a party was to be put. There were cases in which a man's mental faculties generally seemed to be in full vigor, but where on one single subject he seemed to be deranged. A man was possessed, perhaps, by a belief of something absurd which he could not be reasoned out of (what was called an insane delusion), or he might have some morbid propensity seemingly in harsh discord with the rest of his intellectual and moral nature. Those were cases, which, for want of a better term, were called partial insanity. Sometimes its existence and sometimes its limits were doubtful and undefined, and in those cases it was difficult to determine whether the patient had passed the line of moral and legal accountability for his actions.

The jury would bear in mind that a man did not become irresponsible by the mere fact of his being partially insane. Such a man did not take leave of his passions by becoming insane. He might retain as much control over them as in health. He might commit offences, too, with which his infirmity had nothing to do. He might be sane as to the crime he committed; might understand its nature, and might be governed by the motives in relation to it as other people; while on other subjects having no relations whatever to the crime, he might be the victim of delusion. Whenever this partial insanity was relied on as defence it must appear that the crime charged was a product of the delusion or other morbid condition, and connected with it, as effect with cause, and that it was not the result of sane reasoning, which the party might be capable of, notwithstanding his limited and circumscribed disorder. Assuming that that infirmity of mind had a direct influence on crime, the difficulty was to fix the character of the disorder which fixed responsibility or irresponsibility in law. The outgoings of the judicial mind on that subject had not been always entirely satisfactory, nor in harmony with the conclusions of medical science. Courts had in former times passed upon the law in regard to insanity without regard to the medical aspect of the subject; but it would be only properly dealt with by a concurrence of harmonious treatment between the two sciences of law and medicine. The Courts had, therefore, adopted, and again discarded, one theory after another in the effort to find some common ground on which to stand, and his effort would be to give to the jury the results most commonly accepted by the Courts.

It would be well to say a word to the jury as to the kind of evidence by which Courts and juries were guided in this difficult and delicate inquiry. That subtle essence called mind, defied, of course, ocular inspection. It could only be known by its manifestations. The test was as to whether the conduct of the man and his thoughts and emotions conformed with those of persons of sound mind, or whether they contrasted harshly with it. By that a judgment was formed as to a man's soundness of mind. And for that reason evidence was admitted to show conduct and language that would indicate to the general mind some morbid condition of the intellectual powers. Everything relating to his mental and physical history was, therefore, relevant, because any conclusion on the subject must often rest on a large number of facts, and letters, spontaneously written, afforded one of the best indications of mental condition. Evidence of insanity in the parents was always pertinent, but juries were never allowed to infer insanity in the accused from the mere fact of its existence in the ancestors. When, however, there was evidence tending to show insane conduct on the part of the accused, evidence of insanity in the ancestors was admissible as corroborative of the other. Therefore it was that, in this case, the defence had been allowed to introduce evidence covering the whole life of the accused, and reaching also his family antecedents. In a case so full of detail he should deem it to be his duty to call the attention of the jury to particular parts of it, but he wished the jury to distinctly understand that it was their province, and not his, to decide upon the facts; and if he, at any time, seemed to express or intimate an opinion on the facts (which he did not design to do), it would not be binding on them, but they must draw their own conclusions from the evidence. The instructions which he had already given to the jury imported that the true test of criminal responsibility, where the defence of insanity was interposed, was, whether the accused had sufficient use of reason to understand the nature of the act with which he was charged, and to understand that it was wrong for him to commit it. If those were the facts, he was criminally responsible for the act, whatever peculiarities might be shown of him in other respects. On the other hand, if his reason were so defective, in consequence of brain disease, that he could not understand what he was doing, or could not understand that what he was doing was wrong, he ought to be treated as an irresponsible lunatic. As the law assumes every one, at the outset, to be sane and responsible, the question was, what was there in this case to show the contrary as to this defendant? A jury was not warranted in inferring that a man was insane from the mere fact of his committing a crime, or from the enormity of the crime, because the law presumes that there is a bad motive, and that the crime is prompted by malice, if nothing else appears.

Perhaps the easiest way for the jury to examine into the subject was: First, to satisfy themselves about the condition of the prisoner's mind for a reasonable period of time before any conception of the assassination had entered it, and also at the present time, and then consider what evidence exists as to a different condition of mind at the time of the commission of the act. He should not spend any time on the first question, because to examine it all would require a review of the evidence relating to over twenty years of the prisoner's life, and this had been so exhaustively discussed by counsel that anything he could say

would be a wearisome repetition. It was enough to say that on the one side this evidence was supposed to show a chronic condition of insanity before the crime; and on the other side to show an exceptionally quick intelligence and decided powers of discrimination. The jury would have to draw its own conclusions. Was the prisoner's ordinary, permanent, chronic condition of mind such that he was unable to understand the nature of his actions, and to distinguish between right and wrong in his conduct; was he subject all the time to insane delusions which destroyed his power so to distinguish; and did these continue down to and embrace the act for which he is on trial? If so he was simply an irresponsible lunatic. On the other hand, had he the ordinary intelligence of sane people so that he could distinguish between right and wrong as to his actions? If another person had committed the assassination, would the prisoner have appreciated the wickedness of it? Would he have understood the character of the act and its wrongfulness if another person had suggested it to him? The jury must consider these questions in their own mind. If the jury were satisfied that his ordinary and chronic condition was that of sanity —at least so far that he knew the character of his own actions and how far they were right and wrong—and that he was not under any permanent insane delusion which destroyed his power of discriminating between right and wrong, then the remaining inquiry was whether there was any special insanity connected with this crime.

It would be seen that the reliance of the defence was the existence of an insane delusion in the prisoner's mind, which so perverted his reason as to incapacitate him from perceiving the difference between right and wrong as to this particular act. As a part of the history of judicial sentiment on this subject, and by way of illustrating a difference between insane delusions and responsibility, he would refer the jury to a celebrated case in English history which had already been commented on in the argument. Judge Cox here quoted from the opinions of the Judges in the McNaughton case and from some American authorities on the same subject. He went on to say that the subject of insane delusions displayed an important part in this case, and demanded careful consideration.

The subject was treated to a limited extent in judicial decisions, but more was learned about it from works of medical jurisprudence and from expert testimony. Sane people were sometimes said to have delusions proceeding from temporary disorders and from mistakes in the senses. Sometimes they speculated on matters beyond the scope of human knowledge, but delusions in sane people were always susceptible of being corrected and removed by evidence and argument. On the contrary, insane delusions, according to all testimony, were unreasoning and incorrigible. Those who had them believed in the existence of facts which were either impossible absolutely, or impossible, at least, under the circumstances of the individual. A man might, with no reason for it, believe that another was plotting against his life or that he himself was the owner of untold wealth, or that he had invented something which would revolutionize the world, or that he was the President of the United States, or Christ, or God, or that he was inspired by God to do a certain act, or that he had a glass limb —and those were cases of insane delusions. Generally the delusion centered around the patient himself, his rights or his wrongs. It came and went independently of the exercise of will and reason, like the phantasm of a dream. It was, in fact, the waking dream of the insane, in which ideas presented themselves to the mind as real facts. The most certain thing was that an insane delusion was never the result of reasoning, and reflection was not generated by them and could not be dispelled by them. A man might reason himself, or be reasoned by others into absurd opinions and be persuaded into impracticable schemes, but he could not be reasoned or persuaded into insanity or insane delusions. Whenever evidence was found of an insane delusion it was found that the insane delusion did not relate to mere sentiment or theory, or abstract questions in laws, politics or religion. All these were subjects of opinions and were founded on reasoning and reflection. Such opinions were often absurd in the extreme. Some persons believe in animal magnetism, in spiritualism and other like matters, in a degree which seemed absurd to other people. There was no absurdity in regard to religious, political and social questions that had not its sincere supporters. Those opinions might arise from natural weakness, bad reasoning powers, ignorance of men and things, fraudulent imposture and often from perverted moral sentiment; but still they were opinions founded on some kind of evidence, and liable to be abandoned on better information or on sounder reasoning, but they were not insane delusions. An insane delusion was the coinage of a diseased brain, which defies reason and ridicule and throws into disorder all the springs of human action.

Before asking the jury to apply these considerations to the facts in this case he wished to premise one or two things. The question for the jury to determine was, what was the condition of the prisoner's mind at the time when this project was executed? If he were sufficiently sane then to be responsible, it mattered not what might have been his condition before or after; still, evidence had been properly admitted as to his previous and subsequent condition, because it threw light, prospectively and retrospectively, on his condition at the time. Inasmuch as these disorders were of gradual growth, and of indefinite continuance, if he were insane shortly before or shortly after the commission of the crime, it was natural to infer that he was so at the time, but still all the evidence must centre around the time when the deed was done. The jury had heard a good deal of evidence respecting the peculiarities of the prisoner through a long period of time before this occurrence, and it was claimed on the part of the defence that he was, during all that time, subject to delusions that were calculated to disturb his reason, and to throw it off its balance. The only materiality of that evidence was the probability which it might afford of the defendant's liabilities to such disorders of mind, and the corroboration which it might yield to other evidence tending to show such disorder at the time of the commission of the crime. The jury must determine whether, at the time the homicide was committed, the defendant was laboring under any insane delusion prompting and impelling him to do the deed. Naturally they would look first to any explanation of the act that might have been made by the defendant himself at the time, or immediately before or after. Several papers had been laid before them that had been in the prisoner's possession, and that purported to assign the motive for the deed. In his address to the American people of the 16th of June, he said: "I conceived the idea of removing the President, four weeks ago. Not a soul knew of my purpose. I conceived the idea myself, and I kept it to myself. I read the newspapers carefully for and against the administration, and gradually the conviction dawned upon me that the President's removal was a political necessity, because he proved a traitor to the men who made him, and thereby imperilled the life of the nation." Again he said in this address: "Ingratitude is the basest of crimes. The President, under the manipulation of the Secretary of State, has been guilty of the basest ingratitude to the Stalwarts. His express purpose has been to crush General Grant and Senator Conkling, and thereby open the way for his renomination in 1884. In the President's madness he has wrecked the once grand Republican party, and for that he dies." And again, "This is not murder; it is a political necessity. It will make my friend Arthur President and save the Republic." The other papers were of similar tenor. There was evidence that, when arrested, the prisoner refused to talk, but said that the papers would explain all. On the night of the assassination the prisoner had said to the witness Brooks that he had thought over it and prayed over it for weeks; that he was satisfied that he had to do the thing, and had made up his mind and had done it as a matter of duty. He had made up his mind that the President and Secretary Blaine were conspiring against the liberties of the people, and that the President must die. In addition to this the jury had the important testimony of Mr. Reynolds as to the prisoner's statements, oral and written, about a fortnight after the shooting. There he was found reiterating the statements contained in his other papers, and saying that the situation at Albany suggested the removal of the President, and that, as the faction fight became more bitter, he became more decided, that he knew that Arthur would become President, etc.

The prisoner here remarked that Reynold's statement was incomplete.

Judge Cox proceeded to quote from the address to the American people, which was written and given to Mr. Reynolds: "I now wish to state distinctly why I attempted to remove the President. I had read the papers for and against the Administration very carefully for two months before I conceived the idea of removing him. Gradually, as the result of reading the newspapers, the idea settled on me that if the President were removed it would unite the two factions of the Republican party, and thereby save the Government from going into the hands of ex-rebels and their northern allies. It was my own conception, and, whether right or wrong, I take entire responsibility." A second paper, dated July 19th, addressed to the public, reiterated these statements, and added, "I have got the inspiration worked out of me." The jury had now before it everything emanating from the prisoner about the time of the shooting. There was nothing further from him until three months afterwards. And now he would pass to consider the import of all this.

The jury would consider, first, whether this evidence fairly represented the feelings and ideas that governed the prisoner at the time of the shooting. If it did it represented a thing which he (Judge Cox) had not seen characterized in any judicial utterance as an insane delusion. They would consider whether it was evidence of insanity or whether, on the contrary, it showed an ample power of reasoning and reflection on the arguments and evidence for and against, resulting in the opinion that the President had betrayed his party, and that if he were out of the way it would be a benefit to his party and would save the country from the predominance of their political opponents. So far there was nothing insane in the conclusion. It had, doubtless, been shared by a good many heated partizans who were sane people, but the difference was that the prisoner reached the conclusion that to put the President out of the way by assassination was a political necessity. When men reasoned, the law required them to reason correctly so far as their practical duties were concerned. When they had the capacity to distinguish between right and wrong they were bound to do it. Opinions, properly so called, (that is, beliefs resulting from reasoning, reflection, and the examination of evidence,) afforded no protection against the penal consequences of crime. A man might believe a course of action to be right, and the law might forbid it as wrong. Nevertheless, he must obey the law, and nothing could save him from the consequences of the violation of the law except the fact that he was so crazed by disease as to be unable to comprehend the necessity of obedience. [In this connection Judge Cox quoted the decision of the Supreme Court in the Mormon case.] In like manner, he said, a man might reason himself into a conviction of the expediency and necessity of protecting the character of a political association; but to allow him to find shelter from punishment behind that belief would be simply monstrous. Between one and two centuries ago there had arisen a school of moralists who were accused of maintaining the doctrine that, whenever the end to be attained was right, any means necessary to its attainment were justifiable. Consequently, they incurred the odium of nearly all Christendom. By that method of reasoning the prisoner seemed to have gotten the idea that, in order to unite the Republican party and to save the Republic, whatever means were necessary would be justifiable; that the death of the President by violence was only a proper and necessary means of accomplishing it, and was, therefore, justifiable, and that, being justifiable as a political necessity, it was not murder. That appeared to be the substance of the idea which the prisoner had put forth to the world, and if this was the whole of his position, it presented one of those vagaries of opinion (even if it were sincere) for which the law had no accommodation, and which furnished no excuse whatever for crime. There was undoubtedly a form of insane delusion consisting of a belief by a person that he is inspired by the Almighty to do something—to kill another for example—and this delusion might be so strong as to impel him to the commission of a crime. The defendant in this case claimed that he labored under such a delusion at the time of the assassination. His unsworn declarations in his own favor were not, of course, evidence, and were not to be considered by the jury.

A man's language when sincere might be evidence of his condition of mind, but not evidence in his favor of the facts declared by him. He could never manufacture evidence in that way in his own exoneration. The law allowed a prisoner to testify in his own behalf, and therefore made his sworn testimony on the witness-stand legal evidence to be received and considered and given such weight to as it deserved. No verdict, however, could be safely rendered on the sole evidence of an accused party under such circumstances. Otherwise, a man on trial for his life could secure his acquittal by simply testifying that he had committed the crime under a delusion or inspiration, or irresistible impulse. That would be to proclaim a universal amnesty to criminals in the past and unbounded license in the future, and Courts of Justice might as well be closed. He would say a word about the characteristics of that form of delusion. The idea of being inspired to do an act might be either a sane belief or an insane delusion.

A great many Christian people believed not only that events were providentially ordered, but that they themselves received special providential guidance and illumination in respect to their inward thoughts and their outward actions. But this was a mere sane belief. On the other hand, if a man sincerely though insanely believed that, like Paul on his way to Damascus, he had been smitten to the earth and had seen a great light and had heard a voice from Heaven warning and commanding him to do a certain act, that would be a case of imaginary inspiration, amounting to an insane delusion. The question was whether the case of this defendant presented anything analogous to that.

The theory of the Government was that the defendant committed this homicide in full possession of his faculties and from perfectly sane motives; that he did the act from revenge, or perhaps from a morbid desire for notoriety; that he calculated deliberately on being protected by those who were to be benefited politically by the death of the President; that he made no pretence of inspiration at the time of the assassination, nor until he had discovered that his expectations from the so-called Stalwart wing of the Republican party were delusive and that then for the first time he broached this theory of inspiration and irresistible pressure to the commission of the act. Whether this was true or not the jury must determine from the evidence. It was true that the term "inspiration" did not appear in the papers first written by the defendant nor in those delivered to Mr. Reynolds, except at the close of the one dated July 19th, in which he said that the inspiration was worked out of him (although what that meant was not clear), and it was true also that that was after he was informed that he was being denounced by the Stalwarts.

In this connection Judge Cox referred to the testimony of Dr. Noble Young, Dr. MacDonald and Dr. Gray, and this, he said, was about the substance of what was in the case on the subject of inspiration.

The prisoner—Allow me to say that statement by Dr. Gray is incomplete.

Judge Cox went on to say that the question for the jury was whether on the one hand the idea of killing the President first presented itself to the defendant in the shape of a command or inspiration of the Deity, in the manner in which insane delusions of that sort arose, or whether, on the other hand, it was a conception of his own, and whether the thought of inspiration was not simply a speculative or theoretical conclusion of his own mind. If it were the latter, it was nothing more than one of the vagaries of reasoning which he had already characterized as furnishing no excuse for crime. He had dwelt upon the question of insane delusion simply because the evidence relating to that was evidence touching the defendant's power or want of power (from mental disease) to distinguish between right and wrong as to the act done by him. This was the broad question for the jury to determine and was what was ruled upon by the defence.

It had been argued with force, on the part of the defence, that there was a great many things in the defendant's conduct which could not be expected of a sane man, and which were only explainable on the theory of insanity. There were strange things in his career, and whether they were really indications of insanity, or could be accounted for by his ignorance of men, by his exaggerated egotism, or by his bluntness of moral sense, it might be difficult to determine. The only safe rule, however, was for the jury to direct its attention to the one test of criminal responsibility, namely: Whether the prisoner possessed the mental capacity at the time the act was committed to know whether it was wrong, or whether he was deprived of that capacity by mental disease.

There was one important distinction which the jury must not lose sight of, and they must decide how far it was applicable to this case. That was, the distinction between mental and moral obliquity; between the mental incapacity to distinguish between right and wrong and the moral insensibility to that distinction.

In conclusion, he said: From the materials presented to you two pictures have been drawn to you by counsel. The one represents a youth of more than average mental endowments, surrounded by certain immoral influences at the time his character was being developed, commencing life without resources, but developing a vicious sharpness and cunning, conceiving enterprises of great pith and moment; that indicated unusual forecast, although beyond his resources; consumed all the time by unsated egotism and a craving for notoriety, violent in temper, selfish, immoral and dishonest; leading a life of hypocrisy, swindling and fraud; and finally, as a culmination of his depraved career, working himself into the resolution of startling the world with a crime which would secure him a bad eminence.

The other represents a youth born, as it were, under malign influences—the child of a diseased mother, and of a father subject to insane delusions—reared in refinement, and imbued with fanatical religious views; subsequently his mind filled with fanatical theories; launched on the world with no guidance save his own impulses; evincing an incapacity for any continuous employment; changing from one pursuit to another; now a lawyer, now a religionist and now a politician; unsuccessful in all; full of wild, impracticable schemes for which he had neither resources nor ability; subject to delusions; his mind incoherent and incompetent of reasoning coherently on any subject; with a mind so weak and a temper so impressionable that he became deranged, and was, therefore, impelled to the commission of a crime the seriousness of which he could not understand.

It is for you, gentlemen, to determine which of these portraits is the true one. And now, gentlemen, to sum all I have said to you, if you find from the whole evidence that, at the time of the commission of the homicide, the prisoner was laboring under such a defect of his reason that he was incapable of understanding what he was doing, or of seeing that it was a wrong thing to do—as, for example, if he were under the insane delusion that the Almighty had commanded him to do the act, then he was not in a responsible condition of mind, but was an object of compassion, and should be now acquitted.

If, on the other hand, you find that he was under no insane delusion, but had the possession of his faculties, and had power to know his act was wrong; and if, of his own free will, he deliberately conceived the idea and executed the homicide, then, whether his motives were personal vindictiveness, political animosity, a desire to avenge supposed political wrongs, or a morbid desire for notoriety; or if you are unable to discover any motive at all, the fact is simply murder, and it is your duty to find a verdict of guilty as indicted. Or (after a suggestion to Mr. Scoville to that effect), if you find that the prisoner is not guilty by reason of insanity it is your duty to say so. You will now retire to your room and consider your verdict.

During the delivery of the Judge's charge, which was completed at 4.40 P. M., there was perfect stillness in the crowded court room, and even the prisoner kept absolutely quiet, with the exception of one or two simple interruptions. The jury immediately retired, and many of the spectators left the court room.

After the jury had been out about twenty minutes a recess was taken until half-past five o'clock. Many of the audience, who had virtually been imprisoned since 9.30 in the morning, availed themselves of the opportunity to obtain fresh air and lunch. The prisoner, at his request, had been allowed, soon after the jury left the court room, to retire to the little room he had occupied since the trial began as a waiting room during recess. Before leaving the court room he evinced considerable nervousness, but on getting away to comparative seclusion his usual composure and assurance returned to him. He sent out for some apples, with which he treated his attendants, meanwhile chatting familiarly and good-naturedly. He was asked what he thought the jury would do, and replied: "I think they will acquit me or disagree, don't you?" Within ten minutes after the recess had been taken the jury called to the bailiff in waiting that they were ready with their verdict. They were informed that a recess had been taken, and that Judge Cox had left the court room, so they remained in their room until the Court had reassembled.

The rumor that the jury had agreed was quickly spread from one to the other, and the excited crowd surged back into the court room, and with eager expectancy awaited what they all seemed to expect—a verdict of guilty. The musty, antique room is devoid of gas, and the score or more of candles which had been placed upon the desks of the Judge, counsel and reporters imparted a weird and fancifully unnatural aspect to the grim old place. The shadows thrown upon the dark background of the walls seemed like flitting spectres to usher in the sombre procession of those who held in their hands the destiny of a human life.

First came the prisoner with quick, nervous step, and as he seated himself in the dock, perhaps for the last time, the light of a solitary candle fell full upon his face and disclosed its more than usual pallor. Not a tremor of the limbs or a movement of the muscles of the face was observable as he threw back his head and fixed his gaze upon the door through which the jury were to enter.

The Verdict of the Jury.

Judge Cox soon afterward took his seat, the crier called "Order," and the jury, at 5.35, filed slowly into their seats. Every sound was hushed, save the voice of the clerk, as propounded to the foreman the usual inquiry. Clear and distinct came the reply, "We have."

"What is your verdict, guilty or not guilty?"

With equal distinctness came the reply, "Guilty, as indicted."

Then the pent-up feelings of the crowd found expression in uproarious demonstrations of applause and approval.

"Order," "Order," shouted the bailiffs.

Mr. Scoville and counsel were simultaneously upon their feet. Mr. Scoville attempted to address the Court, but the District Attorney shouted, "Wait till we have the verdict complete, and in the due form of law."

Order was at length restored, and the clerk, again addressing the jury, said:

"Your foreman says 'Guilty, as indicted,' 'So say we all of us?'"

"We do," they all responded.

Another demonstration of approval followed this announcement, but not so prolonged as the first.

Mr. Scoville, still upon his feet, demanded a poll of the jury, which was granted, and each juror was called by name, and each in a firm voice promptly responded "Guilty."

As the last man was called, the prisoner shrieked, "My blood will be upon the heads of that jury. Don't you forget it."

Mr. Scoville again addressed the Court, saying, "Your Honor, I do not desire to forfeit any rights I may have under the law and practice in this District. If there is anything that I ought to do now to save those rights, I would be indebted to your Honor to indicate it to me."

Judge Cox, in reply, assured him that he should have every opportunity; that the charge would be furnished to him in print to-morrow, and he would be accorded all the time allowed by law within which to file exceptions, and that he would also be entitled to four days within which to move in arrest of judgment.

Guiteau (who, from the moment Judge Cox began the delivery of his charge,

GEO. SCOVILLE, ESQ., FOR THE DEFENCE.

DISTRICT ATTORNEY CORKHILL.

had dropped completely his air of flippant arrogance, and sat with rigid features and compressed lips), called out, in tones of desperation, "God will avenge this outrage."

Judge Cox then turned to the jury and said:

"Gentlemen of the jury, I cannot express too many thanks for the manner in which you have discharged your duty. You have richly merited the thanks of your countrymen, and I feel assured you will take with you to your homes the approval of your consciences. With thanks, gentlemen of the jury, I dismiss you."

GUITEAU BEFORE THE JURY.

Crying, and Singing a Stanza of "John Brown's Body."

On the day that Guiteau was to read his speech, by permission of Judge Cox, as early as half past eight the doors of the City Hall were besieged for admission to hear Guiteau speak to the jury. It was raining very hard, but still there were thousands of men and women willing to bear it for the chance of witnessing the extraordinary event. An hour before the court was opened every available inch of space was occupied. The close packing of damp garments and the close atmosphere caused intense discomfort, which, however, was unflinchingly borne for the sake of seeing and hearing Guiteau. Everybody seemed impressed with the dramatic side of the spectacle which was about to be witnessed, and, to heighten the effect, the court room was in deep gloom. In fact, it was so dark that very few people saw the assassin when he was brought into court. He came shuffling in sustained by the Sheriff's officers, his hat drawn down over his eyes, and with that furtive, half-frightened look more noticeable than ever during the trial. When he was placed in the dock he gave a quick look around at the great audience. The inordinate vanity of the man was apparent at once, and that this passion was stronger in him even than fear was evident by his change of manner. His counsel, Messrs. Scoville and Reed, his sister, Mrs. Scoville, and his brother, John M. Guiteau, were seated together near one of the tables. Guiteau did not even look at them.

The strain of excitement to which the audience was subjected was manifested in a bustle of exclamation and movement, but as soon as the Marshal's loud voice commanding silence was heard, there was immediate quiet. Guiteau was taken to the witness stand, because it was thought more seemly for him to address the jury from there than from the prisoner's dock. His cheap eyeglasses dangled in front of his coat, and from his pocket a bunch of newspapers protruded. The handcuffs were still on him as he took his seat in the witness box, and he held up his hands to the bailiffs. The audience was so still that the click of the springs was distinctly heard. As soon as the handcuffs were removed the guards fell back again, and Guiteau, looking toward the audience, and not toward the jury, which was on his right, began: "I want to sit down, because I can talk better sitting. I am not afraid of anybody shooting me, because this shooting business is on the decline; but I can talk better in my seat." He spoke in his usual half snappish way, without appearing to address anybody in particular, much as an actor speaks the asides in his part. Drawing a piece of paper from his pocket, and adjusting his eyeglasses, he bent close over the manuscript, but even then he was unable to read it. It was so dark, in fact, that half across the room the assassin could be distinguished only as a human figure sitting there, and in remote parts of the hall people had to be contented with hearing a voice coming from the place where they knew Guiteau was. A couple of German student lamps were lighted and placed near him, and then he read the introduction to his speech.

"The prosecution pretend that I am a wicked man. Mr. Scoville and Mr. Reed think I am a lunatic, and I presume you think I am. I certainly was a lunatic on July 2, when I fired on the President, and the American people generally, and I presume you think I was. Can you imagine anything more insane than my going to that depot and shooting the President of the United States? You are here to say whether I was sane or insane at the moment I fired that shot. You have nothing to do with my condition before or since that shot was fired. You must say, by your verdict, sane or insane at the moment the shot was fired. If you have any doubt of my sanity at the moment, you must give me the benefit of that doubt and acquit. That is, if you have any doubt whether I fired that shot, or as the agent of the Deity. If I fired it on my own account, I was sane. If I fired it supposing myself the agent of the Deity, I was insane and you must acquit. This is the law as given in the recent decision of the New York Court of Appeals. It revolutionizes the old rules and is a grand step forward in the law of insanity. It is worthy of this age of railroads, electricity, and telephones, and it well comes from the progressive State of New York. I have no hesitation in saying that it is a special providence in my favor, and I ask this Court and jury so to consider it. Some of the best people of America think me the greatest man of the age, and this feeling is growing. They believe in my inspiration and that Providence and I have really saved the nation another war. My speech setting forth in detail my defence was telegraphed Sunday to all the leading papers and published Monday morning. Only one mistake occurred in it—my fault. I opened with a quotation from my Christmas greeting to the American people. I omitted to erase the words 'Christmas, 1881,' which appear a few lines from the top of my speech. The sentence erroneously read, 'To-day, Christmas, 1881, I suffer in bonds as a patriot.' And here I desire to express my indebtedness to the American press for the able and careful way they have reported this case. The American press is a vast engine. They generally bring down their man when they open upon him. They opened upon me with all their batteries last July, because they did not know my motive and inspiration. Now that this trial has developed my motive and inspiration, their bitterness has gone. Some editors are double-headed. They curse you to-day and bless you to-morrow, as they suppose that public opinion is for you or against you, which shows the low grade of their humanity. I desire to thank my brother and my sister and my counsel, Scoville and Reed, for their valuable services. I intend to give my counsel ample fees, especially Scoville. He is a staunch man and a hero, and I commend him to the great Northwest as a fine lawyer and a Christian gentleman. We have differed as to the defence. He has his theory and I have mine. I told him to work his theory as he thought best, and he has done it in a splendid way, and I commend him for it. Considering his slight experience as an advocate, he showed himself as a man of marked resources. In other words, you cannot tell what is in a man until he has a chance. Some men never have a chance, and go down in obscurity. There are plenty of brains in this world. Not every man has a chance to develop his brain. It is brain and opportunity under Providence that makes a great man. I return thanks to the Marshal and his aids, to the Superintendent of the Police and his force, to the Warden of the jail and his keepers, and to Gen. Ayres and his forces for services rendered me. I return thanks to this honorable Court and bright jury for their long and patient attention to this case. I am not here as a wicked man or a lunatic. I am here as a patriot, and my speech is as follows."

He took up a copy of the newspaper in which his speech was printed and began to read from it to the jury. He apologized for using eyeglasses, saying that his eyes were weak. Finding that his own did not help him, he borrowed his brother's. These, however, did not suit him, and somebody lent him another pair. These last he snatched from his nose, and then went on without using glasses at all. He rolled forth his sentences in a declamatory manner, holding the paper with one hand and gesticulating with the other. The words, "Rally round the flag, boys," he repeated in a sing-song tone, waving his arm in the air above his head. "And for this I suffer in bonds as a patriot," he quoted in an oratorical manner, and then repeating the sentence, he allowed his voice to tremble so that the words were nearly inaudible. The trembling in his voice continued till he spoke about his mother and declared that he had always been a "lover of the Lord," when he broke down completely, and, applying his handkerchief to his eyes wiped away the tears which naturally or forced for the purpose of exciting sympathy, coursed down his cheeks. He promptly recovered himself, and in his usual tone of voice proceeded with his address.

When he came to the description of the attempts made upon his life by Mason and Jones he stood up for the purpose of the more vividly pointing out to the jury the narrow escape which he had had. With something of pride he held up his arm and showed the rent made in his coat by the bullet fired by Jones, and made his old declaration that it was a proof that the Lord was watching over him. A laugh went through the audience as the prisoner read and re-read his declaration that it would be perfectly safe for him to walk the streets of Washington or New York.

Coming down to the extracts from his mail, he read them with extreme emotion, particularly the rhyming one dated Philadelphia, New Year's Day, 1882, which he read in a sing-song way, which caused a laugh among the audience. He evidently enjoyed the strictures upon the counsel for the prosecution, and his vain-glorious smile was too much for the District Attorney, who joined in the laugh which followed the reading of the extract.

Reaching that portion of the speech where an abstract from his address to the American people is inserted, he folded up the paper, took off his glasses, and squaring himself in his chair, proceeded to repeat the extract from memory. In doing this he assumed his most oratorical style, modulating the tones of his voice, using both arms to aid him in emphasizing his dramatic utterances as far as possible. Coming down to his quotation from "John Brown's Body," he threw back his head and sang a verse from that old song, much to the amusement of his spectators.

He read from his speech:

Put my body in the ground if you will; that is all you can do. But thereafter comes a day of reckoning. The mills of the gods grind slow, but they grind sure, and they will grind to atoms every man that injures me.

And supplemented it with the remark: "As sure as a hair of my head is injured this nation will go down in the dust, and don't you forget it."

The insignificant attempts at eloquence, the ludicrous concert of the man, and the attempt to sing a stanza from "John Brown's Body"—all these would have given the performance an appearance of burlesque had it not been fully realized that the man was the assassin of the President and ostensibly praying to the jury for his life. While he was uttering his ridiculous sentences in his absurd manner there sat the jury within an arm's reach of him, every one of them grim and stern, and the shadow of the gallows, as he went on with his speech, seemed to become more and more distinct. Many who watched the jury thought Guiteau was reading his death warrant. He read about two hours, and closed with a peroration in which he begged the jury not to "get the Deity down on them" by meddling with this case. He begged them for their own sake and for the sake of the American people to let the case alone and let their verdict be that it was the Deity's act. His final sentence was:

When the President was shot his Cabinet telegraphed to foreign nations that it was the act of a madman, and it would be far better every way that it be finally decided that it was the act of a madman.

When the speech ended the court room was as still as if spectators had assembled in front of a gallows. Judge Cox broke the silence by inquiring whether Judge Porter would be able to proceed, and finding he would not, he adjourned the court. The prisoner arose in his box, cast one glance around the audience, tucked his papers in his pocket, and held out his hands to the officers for the handcuffs. His slouch hat was put on his head, and he was led shuffling away to the van to be taken again to the jail. [See picture in this book.]

Now we have, in order to give a straight account, been obliged to omit some very interesting details, which we here present to the reader for the first time.

On the day that the Judge's charge was given to the jury (who returned a verdict of guilty in less than thirty-five minutes) the court room was again densely crowded long before the opening of the court. Counsel were rather tardy in making their appearance, and the court was not declared in session till quarter-past 10 o'clock. Judge Porter entered shortly after 10 o'clock. As usual, the prisoner opened the proceedings by announcing: "My sister has been doing some silly talk in Chicago. She means well, but she's no lawyer."

Judge Porter immediately resumed his argument. Admonished by the falling snow and the severity of the weather, from which he had suffered, and from which, doubtless, the jury also had suffered, he felt it necessary to vary somewhat from his original intentions, and trust to the intelligence and honor of the jury to supply his defects. He would not, therefore, linger over the dry details of the evidence. Feeling it imperatively necessary that this case should be brought to a conclusion as soon as possible, he would simply touch upon a few salient points of the evidence. John W. Guiteau, said Judge Porter, I believe to be an honest man. He came here ready to contribute his means, his evidence and his services to save a brother's life and an honored father's name, and yet the truth comes from his lips, which must impress upon every one of you the conviction that on the 2d of July this prisoner was as sane as you or I, or the Judge upon the bench.

Reading from the evidence of J. W. Guiteau and commenting upon it, Judge Porter said of the prisoner, "he has two faces."

Guitean—How many have you got?

Judge Porter—He has two faces, one showing the sanctity of the Pharisee, and the other the hideous grin of the fiend that possesses him. As he continued to read from J. W. Guiteau's testimony relative to his last interview with the prisoner, Guiteau continually interrupted him with such comments as "What I say is always true."

Proceeding, Judge Porter contrasted the life and conduct, and deceitful, and swindling practices of the prisoner with the Apostle Paul's, in the prisoner's assumption that he like Paul, was honestly engaged in doing the Lord's work, Paul never palmed off brass watches for gold.

"Neither did I," shouted Guiteau.

"Paul never swindled his creditors out of their just dues."

"Oh, you're a blood man," retaliated Guiteau. "You belong to the Judas tribe."

The picture drawn by Judge Porter was anything but a lovely one, and provoked the prisoner to most abusive retorts. "You're a liar, and you know it, and I tell you so to your face, Judge Porter," he called out.

"This man," said Judge Porter, "who says he never deceived any one—["That's a fact," piped the prisoner, "put that in frequently"]—this man who says he never deceived any one, says in one of his handbills, 'Lecture by the Hon. Charles Guiteau.' He never deceived any one! Where did he get this title of Hon.?"

Guiteau—That's the way my letters come addressed, sir.

"By the little giant of the West," continued Judge Porter. "Well, didn't they call Douglass the little giant of the West?" retorted the prisoner.

Judge Porter—Well, I will not comment upon that.

Guiteau—You'd better not; you havne't got brains enough.

Judge Porter—The Lord murdered Garfield.

Guiteau—Yes, and He'll murder you before long.

Judge Porter—The Lord murdered Garfield, the Lord defrauded the printers and the boarding houses, and every night and morning the Christian prisoner thanks the Lord for His work.

Continuing to read from the evidence, Judge Porter was again and again interrupted by the prisoner, who called out, "Read the record. That's bigger than my brother. He's no brother to me and never has been till he came to this trial. It is contemptible in you to speak about my brother in the way you do."

Judge Porter, in an apparently incidental way, spoke of the horror and detestation with which men of all parties and shades of opinion look upon the prisoner, and the unanimity with which they execrate his act.

"You're a liar, and you know it," shouted the prisoner, with the energy of desperation. "The American people are on my side, and so is the press."

As Judge Porter continued his arraignment of the prisoner, Guiteau winced and nervously twisted in his seat, and finally drowned the voice of Judge Porter, who gave way to his clamor. In savage tones he shouted:

"A saint from Heaven couldn't stand the abuse of that man, Porter, and I won't stand it. I will relieve my mind. The idea of that man trying to make me out a fighting man, a man of bad character, and all that. It's a lie, and he knows it. He's a liar, and I'll call him so."

Judge Porter—I am simply giving the sworn statement of his own brother.

Guiteau—He's no brother of mine. I wouldn't have spoken to him at the Fifth Avenue last summer; I have nothing against him, but I don't like his style. I didn't like my father's style either. My sister sympathizes with me, and my brother sympathizes with my father. I want that understood. It's contemptible in that man Porter to undertake to convince that jury that I'm an unprincipled, bad man.

Judge Porter read from a letter of Luther W. Guiteau's, when the prisoner again called out, "Scoville was very smart to put that letter in, wasn't he? It shows what a blockhead he is, anyway."

The first interruption by counsel for the defence occurred when Judge Porter undertook to quote the opinion of the English judiciary upon this case.

Colonel Reed interposed an objection, but, without heeding him, Judge Porter continued his remarks.

Colonel Reed insisted upon his objection.

Colonel Corkhill, springing to his feet, protested against the interruption. "You have made your objection, that's the extent of your prerogative. You've no right to interrupt the gentleman."

Judge Cox—What Judge Porter has said is neither very relevant nor very objectionable. I don't see that you can object.

The prisoner added his comment—Your Honor ought to put that man under arrest. He's a perfect nuisance this morning.

After this outburst Judge Porter continued to speak for some minutes without further interruption.

Alluding to the incident of the watch, Judge Porter arraigned both prisoner and counsel for their contemptuous manner of speaking of the witness Edwards as a miserable Jew. "I have yet to know," said the speaker, "that any man lives who could have cause to feel ashamed that he sprang from the same race as the Saviour of mankind."

The interruptions of the prisoner increased in violence and frequency, till, reinforced by an objection of Mr. Scoville, the clamor and din for a moment resembled a small Babel.

Mr. Scoville finally made himself heard, and desired an exception noted to a statement or construction put upon the evidence by Judge Porter. A sharp discussion ensued, during which the prisoner made himself heard from the dock, shouting, "It's an outrage for that man to be allowed to speak. He ought to be under arrest for his insolence. It has been nothing but one stream of abuse from him all the morning. It's enough to provoke a saint from Heaven. It's a disgrace upon a Court of justice."

The bailiffs undertook to quiet the prisoner and succeeded in drawing his attention from the dispute of counsel and attracting his abuse to themselves. It seemed for a moment more than possible that his vicious demonstrations might provoke some of the officers beyond the point of endurance, and perhaps to the point.

Judge Cox called for the reading from the stenographer's notes of the passage which had caused the dispute, and promptly decided against Mr. Scoville's impetuous demand "that the counsel be stopped."

Passing to the testimony of Dr. Spitzka, Judge Porter said: I wonder if Lucifer were on trial would Dr. Spitzka pronounce him a moral imbecile —a moral monstrosity? Satan fell from a high estate. There was a change in Satan, but in this man, according to Dr. Spitzka, there never could have been a change. He was from the start a moral imbecile—a former of morbid projects— says Dr. Spitzka. Why are the most of mankind poor? Because of morbid projects. Yet do we pronounce the majority of mankind insane? What does he say of the prisoner as a lawyer? He calls him a third-rate shyster in a criminal court. I suppose Scoville can tell you what that means—I cannot—said Judge Porter.

"Well, some of your clients can tell what it is," retorted the prisoner.

Referring to the reference by Colonel Reed to Charlotte Corday, Judge Porter said it was left to Reed to make the discovery, and to announce to this Court and to the world that Charlotte Corday was insane. Rehearsing the circumstances of Charlotte Corday's life and death, Judge Porter contrasted her act of patriotism with Guiteau's foul murder in most eloquent and stirring sentences. The prisoner was aroused almost to fury, and bellowed like an infuriated beast, at times completely drowning the speaker's voice.

"God Almighty will curse you, Porter. You miserable whelp, you; you can't make the American people believe I'm not a patriot. To-day I suffer in bonds as a patriot, and God will curse you if a hair of my head is injured."

Pausing a moment, Judge Porter said: Contrast the conduct of this vindictive cowardly wretch with that of Charlotte Corday, who walked peacefully to the scaffold with hands folded over the crosses upon her breast, and the serene smile that denoted her willingness to suffer death for her country and the patriotism which instigated her act.

"I aint afraid to die, either!" shouted the prisoner. "You may put my body in the ground if you can, but I tell you this nation will go down in blood if you harm a hair of my head."

Next, Judge Porter compared the prisoner to Wilkes Booth, and showed the latter to be almost a patriot, compared with the cowardly assassin now on trial, for Booth was actuated by a mistaken motive of patriotism, and was a man of manhood and manliness. But this sneaking, cowardly wretch, who could plan for his victim's death and his own safety at the same time, murdered his man for revenge and for notoriety.

Guiteau—"I shot my man in broad daylight, and don't you forget it, Porter."

Pressing the assertion that Guiteau was actuated by revenge and a desire for notoriety, Judge Porter compared him to a noted criminal in Europe. I don't recall his name, said Judge Porter; but he said, "I am the ugliest man in Europe."

"Well, you wasn't there," interrupted Guiteau. "You'll be the ugliest man in history, though."

"He said," continued Judge Porter, "I would rather be the ugliest man in Europe and have notoriety, than remain in the ranks of mediocrity."

For the next half hour there was one continued stream of interruptions and abuse from the prisoner. A score of times he denounced Judge Porter as a liar, varying the expressions as adjectives presented themselves. His vindictive disposition showed itself as never before, and for once his cunning was merged in his angry spite, and, as Judge Porter piled up invectives, the prisoner unwittingly emphasized and corroborated the diagnosis of depravity and wicked heartedness which the counsel was, with such telling effect, pronouncing upon him.

"You know that's an absolute, desperate, wicked, devilish lie," finally shouted Guiteau, stammering with rage and nervousness.

At 12.30 a recess was taken for thirty minutes.

After the recess Mr. Scoville gained the ear of the Court to state that he interrupted Mr. Davidge but once, and Mr. Porter on that morning but twice, and each time in a respectful manner. He did not propose to interrupt again unless it was warranted, and he thought he was entitled to more respectful consideration than had yet been accorded him.

Guiteau followed suit with the announcement that he should not interrupt unless it was warranted; but the harangue which he seemed about to start on was summarily cut short by Judge Cox, who commanded him to keep silence.

Judge Porter resumed: There is one man between you and the grave of the slaughtered President who knows whether this defence is a sham or not.

Guiteau—It is a true defence, and you know it.

Judge Porter—The truth will, however, burst forth and reach the consciousness of any one. If from no other source, it will make its way from the murderer himself. Judge Porter then read from a letter of the prisoner's to his father, in which he said, "For years I was haunted with the idea that I was cut out for some great mission, but now I am convinced that it was a devilish delusion, and I renounce my overweening vanity and egotism."

Guiteau—Well, I've changed my mind since then. That was ten years ago.

Later, reading from Guiteau's criticism upon the religious and moral growth of the past six thousand years, Judge Porter said: Could Judas Iscariot himself have pronounced a more sinister judgment?

Guiteau—Judas Iscariot would have employed you as his attorney, you big liar, you.

His whole life, said Judge Porter, was in accord, and all the evidence substantiated the assumption that revenge and the morbid desire for notoriety actuated the prisoner. How thoroughly he had read up the noted crimes, and how familiar he had shown himself to be with their defences. Where did he get that word "remove" with which to soften the too harsh definition of his too hideous crime? From reading Shakspeare, and his models were those characters in whose portraiture the great student of human nature had depicted the very intensity of human passion.

Judge Porter passed to the discussion of the direct issue of the case whether or not the prisoner was insane on the 2d of July. The prisoner himself, he said, does not claim to be insane.

Guiteau—I aint now, but I was on the 2d of July, and for thirty days previous. Transitory mania, that's what I claim.

Replying to this claim, Judge Porter pointed out its absurdity; that, like the stroke of the lightning, all his insanity should vanish in an instant; that it should envelop him completely, day after day, for the purposes of murder; that it still clung to him after the first shot was fired, and only left him after he saw his victim sinking helpless to the ground, and then it "instantly was worked off" and left him a perfectly sane man.

Guiteau—Well, transitory mania was the plea that Sickles got off on, and you was on the prosecution of the case and got beaten on the very same doctrine you are trying to fool that jury on.

Almost every other sentence that was uttered by Mr. Porter was retorted to by the prisoner, until finally Mr. Porter proceeded to close his argument, which he did, as follows: "Gentlemen, the time has come when I must close. The Government has presented its case before you, and we have endeavored to discharge our duty to the best of our abilities. His Honor has endeavored to discharge his. I know that you will be faithful to your oaths and discharge yours. So discharge it that, by your action at least, political assassination shall find no sanction to make it a precedent hereafter. He who has ordained that human life shall be shielded by human law from human crime, presides over your deliberations; and the verdict which shall be given or withheld to-day will be recorded where we all have to appear. I trust that that verdict will be prompt; that it will represent the majesty of the law, your integrity, and the honor of the country, and that this trial, which has so deeply interested all the nations of the earth, may result in a warning (to reach all lands) that political murder shall not be used as a means of promoting party ends or political revolutions. I trust, also, that the time shall come, in consequence of the attention that shall be called to the considerations growing out of this trial, when, by an international arrangement between the various governments, the law shall be so strengthened that political assassins shall find no refuge on the face of the earth."

These were the last words heard by the jury until Judge Cox delivered his mild but able charge, to the twelve assembled men whose verdict was waited for so anxiously by the million. But let us go back to Porter's second and third days' speaking, giving more fully the text of his very dramatic address to the jury in this now world-wide celebrated case.

On the second day of his great speech Judge Porter entered the room by the jurors' door shortly before 10 o'clock, and, bowing pleasantly to the jury, took his place at the prosecution table. As soon as the court was opened he stepped to the space in front of the jury and was about to begin his speech for the day when the prisoner forestalled him, and called out, from the dock, "I desire to say that some crank has signed my name to a letter that appeared in the papers this morning. It was without my au-

The portrait above is authentic. It is copied from a photograph by Edwin L. Brand, No. 212 Wabash Avenue, Chicago. The photograph was taken in the spring of 1881. Guiteau was introduced to Mr. Brand and ordered one dozen of the photographs, which he paid for. He then ordered another dozen, which he did not call for. From one of the last-named dozen this portrait was engraved.

thority, and I repudiate it. I also want to say in regard to a couple of cranks that I understand have been arrested for hanging around here, if they undertake to harm me they will be shot down. I want everybody to understand this."

Judge Porter, who had paused to permit this preliminary announcement, began by saying, "The prisoner, as usual, has made the opening speech."

This whole defence, Judge Porter said, had been a sham and an imposture —an imposture which was supposed to have gained a strength of credence from reiteration. The truth asserted by this defence is that truth which is uttered with effrontery, enforced by persistency, and reduplicated by reiteration. This is the truth which they assert in opposition to that truth which you are to ascertain and declare. In my remarks yesterday I showed you how the prisoner has belied by his acts his profession, how he has belied by his acts the character given him by his counsel. I showed you that he had been a liar, a swindler, a murderer at heart from the beginning. That this man has grown worse every year of his life we have all seen and know.

Guiteau—"That's bosh and you know it, Porter."

Judge Porter continued to depict the character of the prisoner and the fallacies of his defence, when Guiteau again and again interrupted him, at one time calling out: "Attorney General McVeagh wouldn't have anything to do with it."

Judge Porter, half replying to the prisoner, said: "And this Christian gentleman would have you even believe that Attorney General McVeagh had dipped his hands in Garfield's blood."

Guiteau—"Oh, that's very fine."

A moment later an allusion having been made by Judge Porter to the present Attorney General, Guiteau bawled out, "He's a high-toned gentleman and you're a wine-bibber. I've got your record, Mr. Porter."

Judge Porter (with deliberation)—"Well, perhaps I am."

Guiteau (with a drawling accent)— Well, I—guess—you—are, Mr.—Judge Porter."

The first serious outbreak of the morning occurred when Judge Porter, adverting to the statement of the prisoner's counsel and the reiterated assertions of the prisoner himself, that the notes of the stenographer, Bailey, were destroyed by the prosecution because they would have benefited the defence, denied the right of the defence to expect or demand to see papers prepared by the prosecution solely for their own use. Furthermore, said Judge Porter, there was not contained in them anything, as asserted by the defence, that would have improved their standing in this case. Mr. Scoville insisted on being heard, and demanded that the Court should stop counsel from making any such statements on his own authority as to the contents of papers which had not been in evidence before the jury. Judge Porter insisted he had a right to deny statements of the same character made by the other side.

Judge Cox thought the counsel had no right to make any statements as to the contents of such papers.

Judge Porter, with much feeling, protested that he had been a practitioner longer than the Judge, and had never before heard such a ruling. He (Porter) was, of course, debarred from taking a legal exception, but he must protest against the unfairness of the position which would admit all sorts of statements from the prisoner and from his counsel, and yet would debar the prosecution from all opportunity of refutation.

Col. Reed, with considerable excitement, but without rising from his seat, said: "If I was the Judge, I would put him under arrest. Such insolence to the Court should be punished."

Judge Porter resumed his argument, and proceeded to discuss the question of reasonable doubt as an element of the defence of insanity. Referring to the decision of Judge Martin, of New Jersey, which had been reinforced by a decision in Ohio, he was again interrupted by Mr. Scoville, who desired to know if arguments were to be heard again upon the law points. A sharp colloquy between counsel ensued, when Judge Porter removed the objection by handing his authority to the Judge, saying: It will answer every purpose of mine, your Honor, if you should have occasion to rule upon the point.

Returning again to the crime and its commission, Judge Porter said:

Who killed Garfield?

Guiteau—The doctors.

Judge Porter—The doctors?

Guiteau—Yes, the Lord let them do it to confirm my act.

Judge Porter—Secretary Blaine was responsible.

Guiteau—I say morally responsible.

Judge Porter—Mr. Blaine saved his life on that night before the murder simply by his presence with him as they walked together. He might have saved his life on that fatal 2d of July but from the fact that the murderer stole up from behind. Then Mr. Blaine is morally responsible for not preventing the crime.

The prisoner confessed that Mrs. Garfield's presence with her husband on a former occasion had prevented him from shooting.

He was asked if Mrs. Garfield had been leaning upon his arm instead of Mr. Blaine on that fatal morning would you have shot him? and he answered "No." Then Mrs. Garfield is responsible for her husband's death, according to the fallacies of this wretchedly fallacious defence.

Referring to the flight of counsel for the defence, when he painted the President's widow at her daily prayers, praying for the acquittal of the prisoner in the name of justice, Judge Porter showed up the profanity and inconsistency of such assertions and rebuked the assumptions of a man who had never exchanged a word with Mrs. Garfield, in presuming to credit her with such monstrous sentiments. Continuing, Judge Porter said, Who is responsible? John H. Noyes; he is responsible. He killed Garfield. John H. Noyes, from whom the prisoner stole his lectures.

Guiteau—That is false. I rely on my own brains for my productions.

Who else, his father is responsible; that father whom he struck, when eighteen years old, he killed President Garfield; that father whom he says he can never forgive, and with whom he had not for the last fifteen years of his honored life exchanged a word. Who else is responsible? Why the mother; the mother whom he scarcely remembers; who was guilty of the monstrosity of having an attack of erysipelas so as to necessitate the cutting off of her hair some weeks before his birth and who for this reason, it is asserted, transmitted congenital insanity to this murderer. Who else is responsible? Why Uncle Abram, who was drunken and dissolute, but not insane. He transmitted insanity to him, although he did not become insane until after he (the prisoner) was born. He killed Garfield by making the prisoner insane. Who else is responsible? Why Uncle Francis killed Garfield. Uncle Francis, who as we are told, being disappointed in love, either killed the husband of the woman he loved, or fought a sham duel, and long after became demented. He killed Garfield by making this man a congenital monstrosity, as Dr. Spitzka says. Then cousin Abby, she is responsible, who, unfortunately, was taken possession of by one of this Guiteau tribe, a travelling mesmerist, and her young mind so wrought upon that finally she was, for better protection, sent to an asylum. She killed Garfield by making this murderer insane; and, as if all this were not enough to kill President Garfield—

Guiteau—There's enough to kill your case according to your own showing.

Judge Porter—Why the Chicago Convention killed him. If they had not nominated him I should not have killed him, says the prisoner. The Electors killed him, for if he had not been chosen President he would not have been killed. "His nomination was an act of God, his election was an act of God," says the prisoner; and he would have us believe that the Deity, who had thus twice confirmed his choice, found it necessary to correct his labor by appointing this wretched swindler, this hypocrite, this syphilitic monstrosity, to murder the President whose nomination and election He had confirmed. These are the defences put forward by this prisoner and his trained counsel to divert your attention from the fact that the deliberate murderer of Garfield sits there (pointing at the prisoner). But even this is not enough. The press killed Garfield, and the press is arraigned by the prisoner, and, without an indictment, the press is found guilty by the murderer;

but, fortunately, they are found guilty only by the blistered tongue of the murderous liar himself.

Judge Porter denied the assumption of Colonel Reed that President Garfield thought that Guiteau was insane, and quoted from conversations with the doctors to show the weakness of the assertion. Alluding to President Arthur Judge Porter asserted that he was Garfield's successor by the same Constitutional force of legitimacy as was Garfield himself.

Guiteau shouted—Made so by the inspiration of Guiteau, and don't you forget it, Porter.

Replying to a taunt from the prisoner Judge Porter described him as slippery as the orange peel, as venomous as the rattlesnake, and speaking of the act of murder said: "This is a rattlesnake without the rattle, but not without the fangs. I might," said Judge Porter, "detain you a week, but I am here for the purpose of ascertaining whether this man is guilty, and these collateral issues I will not delay upon."

The junior counsel, said Judge Porter, has told you you are kings, implying that you may override law and evidence in grasping an almost intangible doubt, and ignoring the solid structure of evidence of guilt. You are not kings! and the man who told you so is the junior counsel—the only man in fifty million who would or could recommend Guiteau for office. Recess.

After the recess Judge Porter resumed his argument, and by a masterly portraiture pointed out the cunning, the duplicity, the acting of the prisoner, since the beginning of the trial. You are, gentlemen of the jury, no more kings in respect of the law than the prisoner in the dock, who sits uncrowned save with his own conceit. Referring to the oft-repeated assertion that he had sent Garfield prepared to meet his God, and he (Guiteau) too was ready to die if God willed it, Judge Porter, with deliberate emphasis, said: I do not believe in all this vast assemblage there is one soul that contemplates with such abject terror the possibility of facing his Maker as does this brazen murderer. Guiteau whirled around with the ferocity of a wild beast, and fairly yelled, "That's a miserable lie, and you know it, Porter, and you are an infernal scoundrel. I hope that God Almighty will send for you soon, both you and Corkhill, such a miserable, stinking whine as that is." The law, said Judge Porter, as it bears upon this case, is supreme, and you are but simply God-made men, under the obligation of a solemn oath, to bring in your verdict under the law and the facts.

Summing up the questions presented by the case upon which they were soon to be called upon to pass, Judge Porter said: The first of these questions for you to consider is: Was the prisoner insane on the 2d of July; if he was not, the case is at an end and your sworn duty is ended.

Second. If you reach that—if he was insane on that day was he insane to that degree that, on the 2d of July he did not know that murder was morally and legally wrong? If he was not insane to that degree, you are bound under your oaths to convict him.

Third. If, in utter disregard of his confessions, under oath you shall find that he actually and honestly believed that God had commanded him to kill President Garfield, and that he was under a delusion, unless you find the further fact that such delusion disabled him from knowing such act was morally and legally wrong, you are bound under your oaths to convict him.

Fourth. If you find such delusion did not exist, that God commanded him to do the act, and that such delusion was the sole product of insanity, then, and then only you can acquit him, when you find he was unable to control his own will. And you must remember, that under oath he has sworn that he was able to control it, for he said, "had Mrs. Garfield been with him at the depot on the 2d of July, I would not have shot him."

Fifth. If you find that even though he was partially insane it resulted from his own malignity, his own depravity, yet still you are bound under the instruction of the Court to convict him.

Sixth. If, upon the whole case, you have no reasonable doubt whether he was partially or wholly insane, if you believe that he knew that his act was legally and morally wrong, you are under your oaths bound to convict him.

The law, said Judge Porter, is founded upon reason, and it must not be said that an American jury shall override the law and establish a principle which will let murder, and rape, and arson run riot through the land.

Murder has been in the world since the first born of woman slew the second born, and God knowing man's nature inscribed on tablets of stone, "Thou shalt not kill." Human life to Guiteau is of small value. Life, said he, in one of these letters of his, is a fickle dream, etc. "Whoso sheddeth man's blood by man shall his blood be shed," says the Gospel, and against this we have had the gospel of Guiteau.

You are to judge whether the gospel of our Maker or the gospel of the murderer shall prevail. Reviewing the claim of the defence to hereditary insanity, Judge Porter said that Mrs. Scoville dare not say her father was insane. His family physician, who was with him till death, would have known it and yet not one dare kiss the holy book and make oath to such a statement.

This defence is a falsehood, and a part of the imposture and sham that wraps about the whole case. The incident of the axe Judge Porter turns against the defence with telling effect, and this raising of the murderous axe against his own sister, which she in her honesty of soul imagined an indication of insanity, but which, in reality, was but in keeping with the cowardly attack from behind upon his infirm father, and with the devilish depravity which culminated in his murdering the President, this raising of the axe was the only evidence which his sister could recall through her forty years of knowledge of her brother.

Guiteau twisted uneasily and, with some nervous hesitation of speech, called out: "The prosecution are making a good deal out of nothing. They are just using that evidence altogether different from what Scoville intended. He never ought to have said anything about it. It just shows how little sense the Scovilles have got."

The witness Amerling, who exhibited his bank book to the jury to show them that he had three thousand dollars on deposit at home, was very roughly handled by the speaker, as was Dr. North, and their credibility shown to be more than dubious.

Statements of Jurors.

A sense of profound relief was the predominant feeling on the morning following the verdict with all who had been connected with the long drawn out Guiteau trial, with the exception, doubtless, of the prisoner, his sister and his counsel. The severely serious faces of the jury, which through ten long weeks were so closely scrutinized and so often commented upon, had on this day assumed the joyous expression of the school boy who has laid aside his books to contemplate the pleasures of a long vacation. The deportment of the jury through this tedious trial, culminating in a verdict which commends itself to the intelligence and conscience of the American people, was the subject of universal commendation. Many of them had been subjected to positive inconvenience and losses in business, one in particular, a commission merchant, having lost $5000 in one case through his inability to consult or advise with his employes in a certain matter, the details of which were known to himself alone.

The cost of the Government for board and maintenance of the jury was $3,600; and for their pay ($2 per day, for 73 days) $1,752, an aggregate of $5,352 for the item of jury expenses alone. Very little doubt as to the guilt of the prisoner—as indicted—found a lodgment in the minds of the jury from an early stage of the trial, and the final rendering of their verdict was but a matter of form.

As one of them expressed it, "The prisoner's own words and declarations were sufficient to convict him, even if they had not been supplemented by the evidence of his friends. The idea of insane delusion was dissipated by his announcement at the time of the murder of the reasons which impelled him. That is to say: That he formed the deliberate opinion, from reading the newspapers and from studying the political situation, that the death of President Garfield was necessary to save the country. This in itself was sufficient to show an act of his own planning, and not dictated by inspiration or pressure of the Deity. His subsequent and persistent justification of the act because the same results had flowed from it that he had anticipated before the act, confirmed the theory or fact. Had it been in reality the result of divine pressure, why his anxiety to justify his act as the mere agent of the Deity?"

Mr. Scoville was found at the hotel in conversation with a friend from Chicago, and busily engaged in preparing his application for a new trial.

The only really sanguine person is probably the prisoner himself. On the way to the jail, although the van was saluted with a continuous storm of jeers—the news of the verdict had preceded it—the prisoner never once betrayed any serious emotion. He chatted with the driver and guards; said he was satisfied with the charge of the Judge; that it was very fair on the legal points, but that the jury had gone back on him, and brought in a verdict contrary to the evidence. On entering the jail he threw off his coat, and laughingly called out, "Well, boys, they brought in a verdict against me; but I'll get a new trial, and upset all this business. And don't you forget it." He ate his supper as usual and, as far as could be learned, slept soundly last night. The next morning he called for the papers, and, though somewhat thoughtful and disinclined to talk much, maintained that it would all come out right, that Arthur was his friend, and the American people would not let him suffer.

In a conversation with some of the jurors in the Guiteau case it was learned that what had been said all along as to the prisoner ruining his own case was true. They said that his examination confirmed the jurors in the opinion that he was perfectly sane. What little doubt there was as to the responsibility of Guiteau—and there was for a short time during the trial just a mere shadow of doubt—was cleared away by the argument of Mr. Davidge. This argument, it is said, settled the case, and had it been submitted to them at the time the verdict would have been the same.

To the question whether the jurors had seen any newspapers during their confinement, the answer was that even had they had the opportunity they would not have taken advantage of it, for they were determined from the first not to give any cause for complaint, that they would do their whole duty as jurors, and that, as far as their conduct was concerned, there should be no ground for a charge of irregularity. "In fact, we followed the instructions given to the letter," said one. "We have all studiously obeyed the requirements of the oath, and have decided the case solely on the evidence and the law as given us." Another juror remarked: "For seventy-two days we have been kept together, and, except that we have been allowed to see members of our families in the presence of the bailiff, we have heard nothing from the outside world, and have done our duty, our verdict being made after full consideration and with the approval of our consciences."

Foreman Hamilton said that he thought there had been little or no doubt in the minds of the jury since the testimony of Dr. Young, in whose opinion the jury placed much reliance, was given. "We left the court room," he said, "after the Judge's charge, for the jury room, and the indictment was first read in full, so that all the members of the jury could remember in full what he had been trying. We then took an informal ballot, with the result of eleven for conviction as 'guilty as indicted,' but one ballot was blank. The next ballot was taken at once, when the whole twelve ballots were taken for the result that I had the honor of reporting to the Court and to the American people, that I and my conferees had to state that Guiteau was 'Guilty as indicted.'"

Mr. Hineline said: "I want to express my admiration for Mr. Scoville. He had a thankless task, which, under a conception of duty, he performed in the most noble manner. My heart went out in sympathy toward him. At times I thought he would break down under his great burden. My whole heart goes out in sympathy toward him. I regard Mr. Reed also as a strong man. His speech was the speech of the trial."

Mr. Bright said: "I never thought for a moment that he was insane, and yet I am told that I am the man some people predicted would ——— the jury."

Jurymen Brawner and Brandenburg each expressed themselves as having been thoroughly convinced when the testimony was closed that the prisoner was sane.

Mr. Prather said: "I had doubts as to how the rest were going. We agreed from the first not to express or ask opinions, but I had thought to myself sometimes this or that man will hang the jury. I never was more surprised in my life than when the vote came in as it did at first—eleven to one. I had thought that we might be out two or three days, although I was myself convinced by the preponderance of evidence."

Messrs. Langley, Gates, Sheehan and Wormley gave a similar report.

GUITEAU GUILTY.

In this book we had made up our minds to give not one opinion from the entire press of the country, but we are led, at this point of the case, to give to our readers a short editorial from probably the most conservative and "mild-mannered" newspaper in this country, possibly the entire world. We refer to the Philadelphia *Public Ledger*.

"There was at last one creditable feature about the Guiteau trial. The Court, the counsel, the audiences, and some of the witnesses, joined as if in concert with the murderer to disgust the country and shame Americans all over the world; but the jury did its duty in a way and with a result that presents one redeeming point. The jurymen had been the victims of this prolonged trial of everything calculated to break down the spirit and exhaust the patience of men, yet they bore it all with an admirable sense of duty. It would not have been surprising if some of them had been bewildered by the bedlam in which they had been living for seventy-two days, but they kept their minds clear, and the clear mind is in their judgment of guilty.

"For almost as many weary weeks as the people of the country counted the flickering pulse-beats of the murdered President they had to endure the disgrace of this most scandalous travesty of trial for murder. Then it was hope alternating with fear, but with an outpouring of affection surrounding it all with a halo. Since and during the trial it has been gross misbehaviors at the bar, alternating with ruffianism and obscenity in the dock, and helplessness on the bench, with the pestiferous atmosphere exhaled by the assassin permeating it all. They all (except the jury) got poisoned by it. The trial was on but a few days when the court room became a resort as if it was a variety show or a horse race, and this most solemn and profoundly affecting tragedy the country has ever had to witness was degraded into a "roaring farce." There were ten weeks of more disgraceful and humiliating proceedings than any Court in any English speaking country ever beheld. Of all who had to do with the trial, Judge, counsel, spectators, none are free from a share of the just censure due to this, the jury above excepted.

"The trial should not have occupied more than a quarter of the time the country was compelled to endure the shame. Nine-tenths of the testimony was irrelevant rubbish, the shameful license given to the assassin made excuse for a claim of license and the introduction of irrelevant matter on the other side—and both made the pretext for the interminable and equally irrelevant harangues and stump speeches the lawyers called arguments. These were all marvels in the way of showing how weeks may be consumed in torrents of talk to little purpose. Such is the way the ten went by in doing what might have been confined to two weeks and ought to have been kept within three. And in addition to the severe affliction of the country by the assassin's act, this way of permitting the trial to drift at the caprice of the murderer, or rather of allowing it to be conducted by him, has cost the people a vast amount of money which has been a vast deal of waste.

Exhibiting Guiteau's Body. A Plan to Pay off Debts and Give Relief to the Insane.

Mr. Scoville was asked if it was true that he had accepted, on behalf of Guiteau's relatives, the propositions from a firm in Philadelphia to refrigerate and exhibit Guiteau's body and replied at first evasively. "You can say that Guiteau's body is not yet for sale. There is a motion for a new trial pending and after that there will probably be an appeal to the Court in general term to be prosecuted."

"To be sure, you do not think the time has arrived to enter into any contracts of such a nature, but is it true, as alleged, that you look upon such a proposition with some favor?"

"I have no right to dispose of Guiteau's body," replied Mr. Scoville. "It is for his sister and brother to determine what shall be done with it. So far as I am concerned personally I see no reason why such an arrangement should not be made. Of course his family would not consent to any arrangement or any disposition of the body with a view to deriving any pecuniary aid from it. If they should consent to the Philadelphia proposition it would be upon the conditions that a post-mortem examination of the brain should first be made, to determine beyond doubt the disputed question whether or not he has any disease of the brain; then the firm that proposes to exhibit the body would be required to give positive assurance to the relatives that no indignities shall be offered the remains. The proceeds of such exhibition would be used by the family, first, in paying off Guiteau's debts, and the remainder, if any, would be devoted, under the control of trustees, to the amelioration of the condition of the insane or to the advancement of anti-capital punishment theory. It would probably be next to impossible," continued Mr. Scoville, "to bury the remains and protect them from the body-snatchers. They would have more incentive to steal his remains than those of A. T. Stewart and could do so with much less difficulty. Nothing but cremation or sinking them in the ocean would prove effective against this class of speculators, and if they can be made to subserve some worthy philanthropy it seems to me far better to dispose of them in this way."

Mr. Scoville said he had received a few responses to his published appeal and some small contributions.

District Attorney Corkhill declined to say whether the government would take possession of Guiteau's body.

Lawyers outside of the case said that the Government would have authority over the body. The matter of its disposition had not been considered by the authorities, but the supposition was that the body would be delivered to the family if they requested it, as it was not customary in civilized countries to pursue a man after he was dead or in anywise mistreat the body. Mr. Charles Reed, who assisted in the defence of Guiteau, said the proposition publicly to exhibit his body was monstrous and an outrage upon common decency. He said that such a thing would not be allowed; that the person seeking to make the exhibition would be liable to arrest and punishment as a public nuisance.

Argument of the Motion for a New Trial.

When Judge Cox entered the court room on the morning of February 3d, the seats within the bar were all filled, while the space in the rear of the room was occupied by a crowd of men and boys, who stood closely packed together or leaned against the rail.

The prisoner was immediately brought in and placed in the dock.

Before taking his seat Guiteau looked over to his counsel, and said in a quiet and rather pleading tone: "Can I sit at that table if your Honor please?"

Judge Cox—"If there is no objection from counsel."

Guiteau—"Have you any objection, Colonel?"

Colonel Corkhill—"No, sir."

The prisoner then took a seat at the table by the side of Mr. Scoville, and taking out of his coat pocket a roll of manuscript, addressed the Court in the apparent belief and with the air of principal counsel in the case. "If the Court please, before the motion is made, I desire to correct a few errors that have crept in."

At this point he was stopped by the Court.

Col. Corkhill objected to any remarks from the prisoner at this stage.

Mr. Scoville also objected and thought anything of the kind had better be postponed until the business before the Court was disposed of.

Mr. Scoville continued: "If your Honor please, I have contemplated that some additional time should be given for this motion. I also have assurances from a prominent member of this bar that he will assist me next week."

Colonel Corkhill asked, "Who is the gentleman?"

Mr. Scoville declined to give the name at present, except in confidence to the Court.

Mr. Scoville then desired to make a new motion relative to additional grounds that he had discovered for asking a new trial. These grounds, he stated, were unauthorized conversations with the jury by outside parties; and, second, by subsequent admissions of an expert, that he thought Guiteau insane, but did not dare to say so for fear it would injure him in business and in the public estimation.

Mr. Scoville read an affidavit, sworn and subscribed to by himself, setting forth in detail the grounds stated, and added, "I have not prepared the formal motion based upon this affidavit, but presume it will be sufficient if I do so at any time during the day."

Col. Corkhill—May it please your Honor, the time for filing such motions and affidavits has expired.

Judge Cox—Well, we will postpone the consideration of this matter until the motion now before the Court is disposed of.

Mr. Scoville then proceeded to read the affidavits and other papers filed by him, with his motion for a new trial.

F. H. Snyder the maker of the affidavit upon which Mr. Scoville relied mainly to sustain his motion, sat immediately in the rear of Mr. Scoville. Col. Reed occupied a seat at the counsel table upon the left and J. W. Guiteau upon the right of his brother.

The intervening days since the verdict of "guilty as indicted" was brought in had undoubtedly been days of anxiety to the prisoner, and left their impress upon his sallow countenance. The cheek bones were more prominent, the lines about the mouth deeper, and the features had a hard and pinched appearance, such as usually betokens late hours and overwork or indulgence.

During the reading of the affidavits by Mr. Scoville, Guiteau listened attentively, once commenting with "That's doubtless true."

After reading the Snyder affidavit, Mr. Scoville defended both the affiant and himself from the criticisms which he learned had been made by the prosecution.

Col. Corkhill, in reply, said: "Neither Mr. Snyder nor Mr. Scoville are now on trial. When they are on trial in this court, I will attend to them. At present the subject under consideration is whether a new trial shall be granted to the convicted murderer of James A. Garfield. I have stated that the signatures upon the paper which forms the basis of the Snyder affidavit are base forgeries, and I expect to prove them so to the satisfaction of the country. I have never accused Mr. Scoville of the forgery, and never supposed him to be guilty of it."

Col. Corkhill then read the affidavits of each member of the jury, in which they most positively deny ever having seen or read a copy of the *Critic* or any other paper during the time that they served as jurors upon the trial of Guiteau.

Following these was read the affidavit of Norman Wiard, to the effect that he had known Snyder for fifteen years, and, to his knowledge, said Snyder is a thief and forger and blackmailer, and that he (Wiard) would not believe him under oath.

Col. Corkhill also read the affidavits of John L. Sargent, formerly a detective in Washington, and Detective McElfresh, who arrested Snyder several years since on the charge of grand larceny.

Also the affidavit of Geo. C. Curtiss, the bailiff in charge of the room from which Snyder alleges to have taken the copy of the *Critic* with the juror's names upon it. Affiant did not purchase a *Critic* during the trial or have one in his room; that the only persons that attracted the suspicion of the bailiffs or jury were F. T. Snyder, Mr. Scoville and J. H. Hayden. These parties passed their rooms on several occasions without having any ostensible business, and were objects of suspicion to both bailiffs and jurymen.

Affiant further swears that the hour when Snyder swore that he found the *Critic* in the bailiffs' room, he (Curtiss) was there, and the jurors were also in their rooms, and that it was impossible for Snyder to have taken a *Critic* from his room unless he had first placed it there.

The affidavit of A. R. Searle, another bailiff in charge of the jury, was then read. It was of the same tenor as the preceding one.

Also the affidavit of Henry Bragdon, the party alluded to by Scoville in his affidavit setting forth newly discovered evidence, as ground for a new trial.

Bragdon's affidavit set forth that he saw a man in Lafayette Park, as alleged, and remarked of him that he looked like a disappointed office seeker or a lunatic, but he did not know whether it was Guiteau or not.

Col. Corkhill, in conclusion, submitted that the affidavits he had read amply sustained his allegation of forgery and fraud, and, therefore, he would refrain from adding any argument.

Mr. Scoville, in reply, merely denounced the attempt to blacken the character of Mr. Snyder. It was on a par with the letters which had been sent to him (Scoville) impregnated with smallpox virus, and the virus injected into these affidavits (all instigated by the personal spite of one man, Norman Wiard) would go out through all the land, and years might be required to undo the injury that is thus proposed to be done to an honorable man, the peer of any in the court room.

Colonel Corkhill raised a laugh by asking in a tone of innocent inquiry: "You are not speaking of Snyder, are you?"

Mr. Scoville replied, with marked emphasis: "Yes, sir, I am. An honorable man."

He then asked the Court to expunge from the affidavits everything of the character he had described.

Judge Cox replied that the objection was clearly well taken, and that much of the affidavits objected to could not be considered as evidence.

Judge Cox then stated that he could not vary from the well defined rules of practice, as to the admission of affidavits or the time for hearing motions, but, as new questions were submitted in the pending motion, he would take time to mature his decision, and would not announce it until to-morrow morning. He would, however, be pleased to hear any legal authorities that counsel might desire to cite.

Mr. Scoville spoke one hour in support of his motion and cited many authorities. The jury, who occupied the same seats respectively as during the trial of the case, gave the closest attention to the proceedings. The crowd within the court room gradually increased until there was not even standing room, and the doors were barred to further admission by the densely packed throng extending far out into the halls. The prisoner astonished every one by his good behavior. The majority of the audience was composed of strangers and many applications for autographs were handed up to Guiteau. When accompanied with the requisite fee, the request met an instant and favorable response.

Reaching over to the reporters' table, Guiteau whispered apologetically: "It seems mean to be charging for my autographs, but I took in seven dollars and a half yesterday, and I have already got several dollars to-day. If I had done this all through the trial, I might have realized $1,000 with which to employ competent counsel. It's the only way I've got now to make any money, though it does seem mean."

Mr. Davidge, in reply to Mr. Scoville, said the affidavit of Mr. Scoville sets forth what could in no event be anything more than cumulative evidence, and even then is rendered null by the counter-affidavit of Mr. Bragdon, the very man upon whose testimony Mr. Scoville, in his affidavit, says he will rely. Mr. Davidge then discussed at some length the Snyder affidavit. Quoting from one of Moliere's plays, in which his hero exclaims, "What in the devil was he doing in that gallery?" Mr. Davidge said: "Applying it to this case, what in the devil was Snyder doing in that room? [Laughter.] What business had he there any more than in my house or my library? I care nothing for the general character of the man—he is found in the novel and unenviable act of invading the sanctity of a juryman's room. What business had he there? Why did he enter the room?"

Guiteau, who had thus far abstained from taking any part of the discussion, called out: "He said the door was open, and he saw the paper."

Mr. Davidge—Yes, I know, Mr. Prisoner, so are a great many houses—but what would you think of me if I went monsing around private rooms?

Guiteau—If you had been in Snyder's place you would have done the same as he did.

Mr. Davidge continued to discuss the affidavit of Mr. Snyder. It was a very easy thing for any one to have put into the bailiff's room the newspaper in question, with the express intention of having it found there. He (Davidge) considered this evidence of the newspaper of very little account.

This elicited from Guiteau the comment: "Very strong presumptive evidence, Judge, especially with a grog jury that smokes, and drinks and plays cards."

Mr. Scoville replied to Mr. Davidge, and argued that Mr. Snyder deserved praise rather than censure for this conduct. He was not "monsing" around, as the counsel intimated. He occupied a room at the hotel, and in going to and from the office to his room, he was compelled to pass through the hall, opening upon which were the rooms of the jury. Seeing the newspaper through the open door he had, as every honest American citizen should, walked in and took it away in the interest of justice. He (Scoville) expected a decision from the bench upon that point.

Col. Corkhill—Well, you'll have hard work to get it.

Mr. Scoville (with much warmth)—Perhaps that may be the case. It is no new thing to experience difficulties. It all comes from that pressure that will have nothing but hang him, hang him.

Guiteau, with flaming eyes and with vehemence, shouted out: "You may succeed now in your villainous purpose, Mr. Corkhill, but we'll win on the long pull, and don't you forget it. The Lord always wins on the long pull."

Mr. Scoville, continuing, discussed the affidavits of the jurymen, every one of which he said, was based upon the affidavit of their foreman, "and these educated and representative citizens of Washington, like so many school boys or parrots, have put their names to whatever was prepared for them."

Guiteau again called out, with great excitement: "God Almighty will ruin every man that is opposed to us. Only give the Lord time enough, and he will do it."

Mr. Scoville strongly urged the propriety of propounding to the jury some questions. He was not satisfied with their affidavits and thought further light would be thrown upon the disputed matter of the newspaper if this was done.

At the conclusion of his remarks Judge Cox took all the papers in the case under advisement. The jury were requested to be in attendance, which was looked upon by some as an intimation that the Court would accede to Mr. Scoville's request. The Court at 2.40 P. M. adjourned.

Guiteau Sentenced to the Gallows—More Blasphemy from the Wretch—Judge Cox Imperturbable.

On February 4th, 1882, at five minutes past ten Judge Cox entered the court room, and the court was formally opened.

The prisoner took his place in the dock, and did not repeat his request to be allowed to sit at the counsels' table.

Mr. Scoville stated that he wished to say that since the adjournment of the Court he had been informed that Curtis, who made an affidavit relative to the *Critic* matter, was not the bailiff in charge of the room at the time the paper was found; that he had been substituted for a man by the name of Sliner, who was in charge at the time the paper was found, and who was withdrawn by the prosecution. "This man," said Mr. Scoville, "I am told knows about the paper, and I can in ten minutes summon as a witness a party who will say that the man Sliner was heard to remark that if that matter of the *Critic* became known, he (Sliner) would have to jump the town."

Colonel Corkhill objected to the evident attempt to postpone the consideration of this motion. If every bit of hearsay gossip was to be dragged in here, there would never be any end to the question.

Mr. Scoville replied that he did not

ask for a postponement; he simply desired to call the attention of the Court to the information he had received, as showing how important it was to investigate this matter with the closest scrutiny.

Judge Cox Refuses to Grant a New Trial.

Judge Cox immediately began to read from manuscript his decision upon the motion.

Reading from various authorities bearing upon the case, Judge Cox discussed at some length the circumstances attending the finding of the newspaper in the room of one of the bailiffs of the jury in this case:

First. As to the handwriting; there are several circumstances that make it improbable that at least two of the names upon the margin of the paper were written by the gentlemen themselves.

Second. If, as suggested, this paper was lying on the table in the bailiff's room, and gentlemen of the jury, in writing in albums, first tried their pens upon the margin, it would amount to nothing in the face of the sworn affidavits of every member of the jury that they did not see or read a paper at any time during the trial. No one could swear to the fact that the jurors did write upon the paper, while they all swear that they did not, and there is no reason to doubt their veracity.

So far as the discovery of new evidence is concerned, the evidence to be introduced is as to the prisoner's manner and appearance prior to the assassination. If there had been no evidence introduced upon this subject, there might be some force in the request; but a dozen or more witnesses testified on the trial as to his manner and appearance, covering the period of time from March until the commission of the act.

The evidence now sought to be introduced would be merely cumulative, and would not affect the verdict.

As to the expert witness whose admissions after the trial are alleged to have been different from his evidence given upon the trial, Judge Cox said unsworn admissions of this character could never be considered as a ground for overturning a verdict that may have been obtained through the evidence of the very witness who, from a corrupt motive, might seek to reverse the verdict. From all the papers presented Judge Cox summed up: "I am unable to find any reason to grant the motion, which is therefore overruled."

Mr. Scoville—"I would like to note an exception to the ruling of the Court."

Colonel Corkhill—"Your Honor, it now becomes my duty—"

Mr. Scoville—"One moment, please. I would like to file in due form the motion which I referred to yesterday."

Mr. Scoville then filed his motion in arrest of judgment.

Guiteau, who had been permitted to resume his seat at the counsel table, called out: "If your Honor please, I desire to ask if there is any motion that I ought to make to reserve my rights?"

Mr. Scoville tried to prevent his speaking, but he retorted: "Well, I don't want any advantage taken of me. I want to know how much time I shall have to prepare my appeal to the court in banc."

Mr. Scoville—"Please keep quiet; we haven't reached that yet."

Guiteau (excitedly)—"I won't keep quiet. I am here, and I propose to do my own talking."

Judge Cox then informed Mr. Scoville of the rules of practice applicable to the filing of his exceptions, and after this matter had been arranged Colonel Corkhill renewed his motion, saying: "It is now my duty to ask for the sentence of the Court."

Judge Cox (to the prisoner)—"Stand up! Have you anything to say why sentence should not now be passed upon you?"

Guiteau (still sitting)—"I ask your Honor to postpone the sentence as long as possible."

Judge Cox—"Stand up. Have you anything to say why sentence should not now be pronounced upon you?"

Guiteau Stands Up for Sentence and Begins a Harangue.

The prisoner then arose, pale, but with lips compressed and desperate determination stamped upon his features.

In a low and deliberate tone he began, but soon his manner became wild and violent, and, pounding upon the table, he delivered himself of the following harangue: "I am not guilty of the charge set forth in the indictment. It was God's act, not mine, and God will take care of it, and don't let the American people forget it. He will take care of it; and every officer of this government, from the Executive down to that marshal, taking in every man on that jury, and every member of this bench, will pay for it; and the American nation will roll in blood if my body goes into the ground and I am hung. The Jews put the despised Galilean into the grave. For the time they trimphed, but at the destruction of Jerusalem, forty years afterward, the Almighty got even with them. I am not afraid of death. I am here as God's man. Kill me to-morrow if you want. I am God's man and have been from the start."

Judge Cox Pronounces Sentence.

Judge Cox then proceeded to pass sentence, addressing the prisoner as follows:

"You have been convicted of a crime so terrible in its circumstances and so far-reaching in its results that it has drawn upon you the horror of the whole world and the execrations of your countrymen. The excitement produced by such an offence made it no easy task to secure for you a fair and impartial trial; but you have had the power of the United States Treasury and of the Government in your service to protect your person from violence and to procure evidence from all parts of the country. You have had as fair and impartial a jury as ever assembled in a court of justice. You have been defended by counsel with a zeal and devotion that merit the highest encomium, and I certainly have done my best to secure a fair presentation of your defence. Notwithstanding all this, you have been found guilty. It would have been a comfort to many people if the verdict of the jury had established the fact that your act was that of an irresponsible man.

"What motive could have induced you to this act must be a matter of conjecture. Probably men will think that some fanaticism or morbid desire for self-exaltation was the real inspiration for the act. It would have left the people the satisfying belief that the crime of political assassination was something entirely foreign to the institutions and civilization of our country; but the result has denied them that comfort. The country will accept it as a fact that that crime can be committed, and the Court will have to deal with it with the highest penalty known to the criminal code to serve as an example to others. Your career has been so extraordinary that people might well at times have doubted your sanity. But one cannot but believe that when the crime was committed you thoroughly understood the nature of the crime and its consequences, (Guiteau—'I was acting as God's man,') and that you had moral sense and conscience enough to recognize the moral iniquity of such an act. (Prisoner—'That's a matter of opinion.') Your own testimony shows that you recoiled with horror from the idea. You say that you prayed against it. You say that you thought it might be prevented. This shows that your conscience warned you against it; but, by the wretched sophistry of your own mind, you worked yourself up against the protest of your own conscience.

"Your own testimony seems to controvert the theories of your counsel. They have maintained, and thought honestly, I believe, that you were driven against your will by an insane impulse to commit the act; but your testimony showed that you deliberately resolved to do it, and that a deliberate and misguided will was the sole impulse. This may seem insanity to some persons, but the law looks upon it as a wilful crime. You will have due opportunity of having any error I may have committed during the course of the trial passed upon by the court in banc, but meanwhile it is necessary for me to pronounce the sentence of the law—that you be taken hence to the common jail of the District, from whence you came, and there be kept in confinement, and on Friday, the 30th day of June, 1882, you be taken to the place prepared for the execution within the walls of said jail, and there, between the hours of twelve M., and two

e. m., you be hanged by the neck until you are dead. And may the Lord have mercy on your soul."

Guiteau's Parting Outbreak.

During the reading Guiteau stood apparently unmoved and with his gaze riveted upon the Judge, but when the final words were spoken he struck the table violently and shouted: "And may the Lord have mercy on your soul! I'd rather stand where I do than where that jury does and where your Honor does. I'm not afraid to die. I stand here as God's man, and God Almighty will curse every man who has had a part in procuring this unrighteous verdict. Nothing but good has come of Garfield's removal, and that will be the verdict of posterity on my inspiration. I don't care a snap for the verdict of this corrupt generation. I would rather a thousand times be in my position than that of those who have hounded me to death. I shall have a glorious flight to glory, but that miserable scoundrel, Corkhill, will have a permanent job down below, where the devil is preparing for him."

After apparently talking himself out, the prisoner turned to his brother, and, without the slightest trace of excitement, conversed for some minutes before being taken from the court room.

The van in which Guiteau was taken from the court house to the jail reached its destination without accident or incident. The prisoner remarked, as he stepped out: "This is a regular Western snow-storm; it reminds me of Chicago."

The Death Watch.

He was taken at once to his cell, and a guard was placed over him. This precaution is always observed in the case of prisoners under sentence of death, and rigidly adhered to in Guiteau's case, both by night and by day. The jail officials, however, did not believe there was the slightest danger of any attempt on his part at suicide—at least until after the review of the case by the court in banc.

All sorts of wild rumors were circulated that Guiteau had killed himself on the way to the jail; that he had hung himself in his cell; that he had taken poison, which had been furnished him by some means unknown to the guards, and other groundless stories, all of which had been rumored several times before. Guiteau himself scorned the idea of suicide, which would detract altogether too much from the imperishable halo which he believed would enshrine his memory as a martyr in the event of the sentence of death being executed upon him.

A Talk with the Assassin— How He Spent Sunday in His Cell.

Guiteau's only visitors were his brother and our correspondent; the heavy snow that had fallen during twenty-four hours having deterred even curiosity hunters from venturing to take the long trip across the commons leading to the jail. The prisoner was found perfectly composed. He said that he had enjoyed a refreshing sleep, besides eating two meals and was hungry for the third. His food was prepared for him by a cook detailed for the purpose, who carried it into his cell, thus preventing any third party's interference. Warden Crocker announced his intention of keeping the strictest watch and guard over the prisoner to prevent any attempts at suicide, although this was scoffed at by the guards at the jail.

Guiteau was one of the first prisoners up and busied himself in tidying up his cell, which is the one he occupied since he was shot at by Sergeant Mason. When he arose from his cot to receive his visitors no one who was not aware of his condition would for one instant have thought him a man under sentence of death, for his manner was gay and careless and he smiled broadly as a reference was made by his brother to his not having dressed himself, as had been his custom for several Sundays, in his best attire and white shirt.

"I don't suppose it makes much difference how I look now," was his reply; "I have weightier matters to think of than dress."

After he was told of Mr. Scoville's trip to New York he seemed perplexed for a moment and questioned his brother very closely as to what was sought to be accomplished by such a move. When John Guiteau said that pressing business and personal affairs required the trip the prisoner angrily exclaimed:

"I don't think he ought to allow any business whatever to interfere with my case and he had better devote his time exclusively to me till after the hearing before the court in banc."

Reading His Bible.

Turning to the correspondent he said: "What is the general opinion outside in relation to the sentence? Don't you think the Judge was a little too hasty?"

As he didn't receive a very comforting answer the prisoner went to the other end of his cell, and turning down the covering from his cot took out a copy of the Bible and began to read it.

"That is his invariable solace when anything goes wrong with him," said General Crocker, "to pretend to be reading his Bible. I don't believe, however, that he pays much attention to what it teaches, except that during the past two or three days he has been more tractable and quiet. He is generally very orderly, but once in a while he becomes excited at some alleged bad treatment from his attendants, but it soon passes off, and he usually apologizes to me for his actions when I go in to see him. His appetite has never failed him but once since he has been confined here, and that was the day after the verdict of the jury. This morning he had for breakfast steak, fried potatoes, bread and butter, and coffee, and for his dinner to-day roast beef, boiled potatoes, and brown bread."

"It was a good meal, too," interrupted John Guiteau, "and when I saw him enjoying it so much it made me hungry, too, and I was compelled to stay and dine with General Crocker. I have put in a pretty good day here talking over family affairs. I came here about eleven o'clock this morning and it is nearly five now."

"Did Mr. Scoville see the prisoner before he left the city?"

"Not since yesterday," replied Mr. John Guiteau. "He did not think it was necessary for him to come over here again to-day, as he had done all in his power for his client and was in a hurry to get to New York."

The prisoner during the conversation was apparently intently engaged in reading, but it was observed that he did not for an instant lose anything that was transpiring around him. The allusion to his appetite seemed to please him, for a broad grin overspread his features when his brother referred to the influence his appetite had exerted over him. As his visitor left the cell the prisoner threw aside his book and followed him to the grating and said:

"Don't forget to let the people know that I am perfectly free from excitement and never felt better in my life. I am trusting in the Deity and the court in banc for a deliverance from this cell and have no fears as to the result."

Mr. Scoville Leaves the City.

Mr. George Scoville was encountered earlier in the day while plunging around through the snow doing a number of small errands preparatory to leaving for New York. He said he wanted a change of scene and thought he could work better away from Washington. Besides, he had relatives in New York, Brooklyn, Albany, and Springfield, and intended visiting them. When asked what would be the next move in the Guiteau case he replied that nothing remained to be done except the filing of the bill of exceptions, and he had ample time to prepare it. He would not have to submit it before the new term of the Criminal Court, which would open on the 4th of March. But if that was not time enough the term might be extended to accommodate him. He said also that he was not certain that he would return to Washington, for when he had prepared the exceptions he could send them to Mr. Reed or to the District Attorney. It was not necessary for him to be on the ground, and he had other work to do which he thought would keep him busy. Referring to the reception of infected letters he said that in company with General Crocker he had waited upon the postmaster in this city and instructed him not to deliver any more letters for Guiteau. He said he would also suggest that the Postmaster General give orders to postmasters not to receive any more letters to "Charles J. Guiteau."

"People will come to think as I do," said Mr. Scoville, laughing, "that Guiteau is half fool and half crazy. The idea of his advertising himself in his last address as though he were a professional beauty. He says also that he don't want anything more printed about him, but if he saw something in a paper to-morrow that he thought required an answer, he would promptly publish another address. He does not remember what he wants or what he has done. He told the doctor yesterday that he had never been vaccinated, but upon examination he was found to have five scars on his arm."

A part of the business that called Mr. Scoville to New York was to arrange for the publication of a book on the Guiteau trial and he also expected to lecture on this great case.

Preparing Guiteau's Scaffold.

How we forget (?) But have we forgotten the cowardly assassination of James A. Garfield?

On the 5th of February, 1882, all preparations were made at Washington, D. C., for the "complete taking off" of our late President's assassin. But let our own correspondent at Washington tell it in his own way:

"The scaffold is standing in the north wing of the jail and has been painted a drab shade. It is of Georgia pine and stands twenty-one feet in height. The cross beam is six by eight timber (strengthened by a heavy top piece for double work), supported by timbers eight inches square. The platform is thirteen feet from the ground and is made of two-inch boards, on stout joists, morticed and bolted, and is eleven feet square. It is supported by six eight-inch uprights in addition to those supporting the cross beam. About three and a half feet above the platform there is a surrounding rail. The trap is five feet square, framed in the centre of the platform, and is flush with it. It is attached to the platform by two heavy strap hinges and is held in place by the ends of the U shaped iron. At the bottom of the iron is attached a small but strong rope passing over a pulley at the back of the structure into a box about four inches square, through which the rope runs into one of the cells, where some person, unknown to the outsiders, at the signal from the warden (usually a motion with a handkerchief) gives the fatal pull. The platform is reached by a flight of steps with a railing on either side.

"To complete the structure and make it ready for use it is necessary that the rope should be attached and the hinges oiled. For a single hanging it is customary to use a rope of manilla seven-eighths of an inch in diameter and thirty feet long. It is not the custom here, as in some cities, to use a rope specially made for the purpose and have it prepared outside the building, for the officers of the occasion. In fact, with the exception of the manufacture of the rope and the iron the structure has been made in the building. There are on hand now several ropes purchased for hanging purposes, and recently several have been received at the jail contributed by persons anxious to have them used on Guiteau. When it is necessary to 'rig' the scaffold a rope will be selected and the hangman's knot will be made by one of the guards, who is quite an expert at it. Then it will be run through the centre hole of the cross beam, thence to the side, passing down one of the uprights to a cleat on the side, where it will be made fast. Generally the slack is four to six feet, and commencing near the knot the rope is for three or four feet anointed with soap, that it may slip easily. In some parts of the country tallow or other grease is used, but General Crocker and his associates prefer the soap. There is also on hand a full supply of small rope to use in pinioning the arms and legs of the victim of the law, and black caps to draw over his face. It is customary to rig the rope the day before the execution and test it by letting drop a bag of sand weighing from 30 to 50 per cent. more than the doomed man. Never having met with an accident or mishap in hanging, the jail officials look on this test as almost useless; but it is always made as a matter of precaution. To make sure, however, of carrying out the sentence within the hours specified therein (usually two hours being allowed), the prisoner is brought on in time to allow fifteen or twenty minutes for services prior to the trap being sprung, and with thirty minutes or more to spare beside. Thus, should there be a mishap of any kind, there would still be ample time to prepare and rig another rope if necessary."

The above is from our "Special" sent on to Washington in the interests of the millions who buy our books. That we have given all a complete account who can deny? Or if denying who can prove? We give you a clean, clear, running history and invite denial.

Guiteau "rises to object," gets off his "funny remarks," and is requested to "sit right down again." Showing the great patience of Judge Cox.

Guiteau „erhebt Einwand," macht einige „seiner scherzhaften Bemerkungen" und setzt sich auf Geheiß sofort wieder auf seinen Platz. Ein Beweis für die Lammesgeduld des Richters Cox.

www.ingramcontent.com/pod-product-compliance
Lightning Source LLC
Chambersburg PA
CBHW020859160426
43192CB00007B/998